DENNY BRAUER'S

WINNING TOURNAMENT TACTICS

with
Monte Burch

DENNY BRAUER'S WINNING TOURNAMENT TACTICS

Photo credits:
  Front Cover; Monte Burch
  Back Cover; Joan Burch
  Gerald Crawford; pages 171, 184, 191
  Ranger Boats; page 182
  All other photos by Monte Burch
All drawings by Monte Burch
Editing, design and typesetting by Joan Burch
Published by:

OUTDOOR WORLD PRESS, INC.
P. O. Box 278
Humansville, MO 65674

First Printing, 1991, Second Printing, 1994, Third Printing, 1996
Printed in the United States of America
Library of Congress Catalog Card Number: 90-92337
ISBN 1-879206-15-3

CAUTION: The techniques and tactics in this book may require technical knowledge, some special abilities, and considerations to safety. The authors and publisher accept no responsibility for the results resulting in the use of the techniques described in this book and disclaim all liability for any consequential injuries or damages. State and local fishing laws may vary. Check regulations before fishing.

DEDICATION

I would like to dedicate my first book to my lovely wife, Shirley and my son, Chad. Without their support and love my career would have never reached this level of success. Also to the bass fishing fans who have helped make our sport what it is today.

ACKNOWLEDGEMENTS

I wish to acknowledge the contributions of some people that helped with my career and also the knowledge that made this book possible.

First to Forrest and Nina Wood for all their friendship and support throughout my whole career. Also to those special fellow competitors who have taught me so much and made life on the tournament trail fun. Larry Nixon, Tommy Martin and others have been good friends as well as great contributors. I also want to acknowledge the special industry people and sponsors for their involvement and last, but not least, Monte for making this book a reality.

Would also like to thank Gerald Crawford, Photographer for BASS Inc. for the Bass Tournament photos.

FOREWORD

From a young bricklayer in Nebraska to one of the countries top professional bass anglers living in the Ozarks of Missouri, Denny Brauer has indeed come a long way, surpassing even his greatest dreams. Spend a little time in a bass boat with him and you'll quickly discover how dedicated he is to the sport of bass fishing. You'll also learn a great deal about catching bass, and you may even hear a funny tale or two. Denny is one of the most concentrated anglers on the professional bass anglers circuit, but also thoroughly enjoys his fishing day, even during the pressures of tournament angling.

Denny has won around $1,000,000 since 1982 until the time of this writing. He is currently third in the B.A.S.S. all time tournament winnings with close to $800,000 in winnings from B.A.S.S. alone. This has all been accomplished in a lot less time and in fewer tournaments than many of the anglers above him in winnings. Denny is just getting started!

In addition to countless money wins and finishing in the top 10, Denny has won an impressive number of titles and tournaments. A listing of major tournament wins to the date of this book printing follows:

1978 Nebraska B.A.S.S. State Federation Tournament
1980 Nebraska B.A.S.S. State Federation Tournament

1984 B.A.S.S. Texas Invitational
1985 B.A.S.S. Tennessee Invitational
1985 U.S. Bass Invitational (Table Rock)
1985 U.S. Bass Invitational (Lake of the Ozarks)
1985 U.S. Bass Angler of the Year
1985 National Match Bass Fishing Champion
1986 B.A.S.S. Texas Invitational
1987 B.A.S.S. Super Invitational (Tennessee)
1987 B.A.S.S. Angler of the Year
1990 B.A.S.S. Tennessee Pro-Am
1990 ESPN Bass & Golf Champion
1991 ESPN Bass & Golf Champion
1992 B.A.S.S. MegaBucks Champion
1993 B.A.S.S. Invitational
1993 B.A.S.S. SuperStars Tournament of Champions

A true sportsman and lover of the outdoors, Denny is just as much as home in the woods hunting whitetail deer as in a bass boat, and just as good with a shotgun as a fishing rod.

He's also a dedicated family man and just as quick to give a youngster an autograph as he is with his mischievous smile.

Perhaps you'll indeed draw Denny Brauer as a fishing partner one of these days, or get a chance to share a boat with him. But if you don't, this book is the next best thing. If you love bass fishing, you'll thoroughly enjoy Denny's excellent advice and amusing anecdotes. If you desire to become a tournament angler, his advice can be invaluable.

Good Fishing!

TABLE OF CONTENTS

Consistently winning bass tournaments requires dedication, concentration, a high degree of competitiveness, and attention to details.

Chapter I

FINDING BASS THE PROFESSIONAL WAY

Seasonal Factors and Patterns

A complete understanding of the seasonal habits of the bass and its lifestyle can help you understand the patterns available in pursuing and catching it. It's best to break this down into the seasons of the year; winter, spring, summer and fall. It is also best to keep in mind the area you are fishing or planning to fish. As an example, winter in Florida differs from winter in the midwest.

A classic example of seasonal movements on Lake of the Ozarks, my home lake, would be as follows--In the winter the majority of bass would be on the deeper bluffs and steeper banks. As the water warms toward spring, they would move toward the chunk rock or rip-rap type banks. As spring arrives and the water temperature rises even more, they would move to the protected gravel spawning areas. With continued warming water, the post spawn and summer fish would pull out again and use the steeper banks. In the fall with cooling down water, they would move back on the flats in force and into the creeks feeding heavily on the forage before winter. With more cooling temperatures, they would pull back onto the bluffs and steeper banks they winter on and the process starts all over again.

WINTER

Winter over most of the country brings a decrease in fish and fishing activity. The colder water slows the metabolism of the bass and less feeding activity is required. Because of this bass movements are more confined and pinpointing holding areas is even more important.

Bass can almost always be caught but your techniques must be adjusted. A good train of thought to maintain is, "The colder the water, the slower you need to fish and fewer patterns will be available that work. The warmer the water, the faster you can fish and there are more patterns that work."

Winter water temperatures can range from 50 degrees down to 39 degrees, and back up to 50 degrees.

Lures that have worked well for me during winter situations are jigging spoons, the jig and pork frog, grubs, tube baits, and free-falling single spins. On the front edge of winter, the single spin is best as shad and forage dies off because of the dropping water temperature. Fish it on the fall, letting it freefall on a semi-slack line down into the zone where the fish are holding. Make it act like a dying, fluttering bait fish.

On the back side of winter, as some bass start to become a little more active, the grubs and tube baits are great, especially on suspended bass. So are the bigger stickbaits like the Spoonbill Rebel. Work them under the water, in stop-and-go retrieves, next to heavy cover that is near deep water.

Winter bass can be caught over most of the country in lakes that do not freeze over. The key is to concentrate a little deeper on the steeper banks. Think slow. Bass still have to eat although their metabolism is much slower. Slowing down is the biggest single key to wintertime success. Any warming trend, even the slightest, can cause an increase in bass activity.

Bass can be caught all winter on lakes that don't freeze over, but it does take some special skills, techniques, and patience. The key is to fish slow.

SPRING

Springtime brings about my favorite season for bass fishing. It is also the time of the year when the majority of quality bass and fishermen make the most contact. By far most fishermen are at their best in water 10 feet and shallower. In the spring bass also spend most of their time in this zone and contact is more easily made.

The bass's main mission in the spring is feeding and getting ready for the spawning cycle. Spring can be broken down into three parts; pre-spawn, spawn, and post spawn. It is very important to be aware of what stage the fish are in and adjust your patterns and techniques accordingly. Bass may even be in all three stages depending on where you fish on a given lake. In a tournament I usually hunt for the pre-spawn, heavier, more aggressive fish. In early spring hunt for bass on the sheltered flats next to deep water. Usually the areas located on the north side of an impoundment warm up faster because of added sunlight exposure. Start there and keep an eye on your water temperature gauge.

When water temperature reaches 45 degrees and the weather is stable, fish start moving shallow. Normally we are looking at 50 to 55 degrees for the good movements to start, with 55 to 70 degrees the prime temperature zone. These temperatures vary somewhat from area to area but are a good guide. Keep in mind that with the cooler water pre-spawn fish, their main objective is to feed heavily and slowly work toward their spawning areas. This is the time of year bass love to hunt crawdads around chunk rock, rip-rip banks, and other places.

Casting the jig-and-frog on these banks and working it in slow hopping and swimming movements can be very successful and account for some huge bass. Also be prepared to

Once the spring water temperature reaches 55 degrees, bass go on a pre-spawn feeding binge. It's a great time to toss a pig and jig or crawdad type crankbait in and around chunk rock banks as well as rip-rap areas where crawdads are abundant.

flip a jig into any heavy cover around these banks, especially if a cold front moves through.

Another bait that is great for these early feeders is a crawdad colored crankbait. Work it slow and stop it now and then as cold water bass have a tendency to follow a lure for some time before taking it. By stopping it you almost force them to bite. On sunny days some bass move shallow against the banks and you can have success with parallel retrieves.

As the water continues to warm, concentrate more on the areas that the bass will use to spawn. Work these areas and usually you can find and catch the big sows that have moved in to spawn. At times they will hold in any cover available just off the spawning area waiting for everything to get just right. Look for this cover or break if bass aren't in the spawning area itself. Since the water has warmed up some, more options become available as far as working lures and patterns.

One of the best days I ever had was when I found the big sows laying in manmade brush piles right off of gravel spawning areas on Lake of the Ozarks. In one day I caught 14 bass between 5 and 9 pounds on Zara Spooks worked slowly over these piles. It was a day when you could actually predict where your next big bite would come.

This is also a great time for flipping and pitching to heavy cover on the spawning banks, especially with off color water and a late spring cold front. Spinnerbaits can also be dynamite worked in these areas, as can buzz baits, if the weather is stable.

As the bass actually move onto the beds to spawn, your techniques also must change for consistent success. I have mixed emotions about fishing for bedding bass and probably won't go into as much detail about how to catch them as I could. I am a firm believer in catch and release but it is never more important than at this particular time of year. A couple of professional fishermen have built careers on their ability to aggravate bedding bass into biting. Hopefully their techniques and methods can be down played so that the majority can enjoy catching bass in the traditional manner. It would be a shame if people not interested in releasing bass would become experts at catching them off the bed. Hopefully the information I give you will be used with the welfare of the bass in mind.

Keep in mind that water clarity normally determines how deep a bass will spawn. With good sunglasses you can occasionally spot the bed and the bass and with patience, agitate it into biting. Tube lures, lizards, and plastic worms all work well when the bass are spawning. A Zara Spook or minnow type bait twitched over the bed can also be good.

The key during spawning season is making repeated casts to objects rather than just one cast. Also spend time with plastic lizards, both Texas rigged and rigged to float. Fish the floating bait in a twitching motion by the cover targets. On some lakes where the bass move onto midlake ridges, flats, and humps to spawn, the lizard rigged Carolina style can be deadly. A friend of mind, former Classic Champion, Stan Mitchell, used this technique to catch a 25 pound stringer at Guntersville Lake during a BASS tournament. He positioned the boat in deep water and worked the Carolina rigged lizard slowly across a three foot deep ridge for the big spawners.

Plastic crawdads and vibrating baits like the "Spot" can also be productive on these flats and high spots. Toledo Bend and Sam Rayburn are classic examples of lakes which have lots of this type of structure.

I am sure it has become obvious that lots of methods can work this time of year. A good example was a tournament I fished on Toledo Bend in the 1980's in early spring. I fished with absolutely the least experienced fishing partner I've had and he literally loaded a boat. He started out with a huge spinnerbait, arched in a 40 foot high cast. It hit the water with a loud splash and a bass jumped all over it. He caught another in the same manner. I was fishing with a pig-and-jig. He had never fished with one, so I tied one on for him and showed him how to fit the pork on the hook. He tossed it out and as I fished I noticed he was watching me like a hawk. When I asked him what the problem was he replied he had never fished with a jig before and what should he do with it. "You better set the hook," I exclaimed as his line went past the front of my boat. It went like that all day, and he ended up with 34 pounds of fish while I came in with four. It was a very humbling experience.

After the spawn comes a period a lot of fishermen dread, post-spawn bass. Actually not all fish are in the same stage at the same time so this saves us on occasion. Post spawners can be caught, and certain methods are very productive.

Jerkbaits can be great around spawning areas with the Bomber Long A and the A.C. Shiner being a couple of my favorites. Lots of these bass, especially the males, are guarding the fry and can be intimidated into striking the jerkbait. You can also pitch jigs or worms in any swarm of fry and get lots of vicious strikes. Most of the better fish back off the spawning areas to the first cover or breakline and suspend. A great technique for these fish is the plastic worm rhythm method.

Twitch and swim it through these areas and you will be amazed at how active some of these post spawners really can get. A lot of these fish are just cruising and are easily caught.

The Spook and Pop-R can also be good. The Pop-R can be great if there are grass lines of milfoil or hydrilla that the bass pull to after spawning. Work it in an erratic motion and concentrate on the shoreline side of the grass beds and lines.

Some of these same grass beds and grass lines can also be places where post spawn fish end up in their summer pattern. Except during the summer pattern they would move to the deep side and the places where the grass tapers off into deep water or butts up against a creek and drops off. These same types of points and creek channels can also be great even if vegetation does not exist on your lake.

SUMMER

Usually the clearer the lake, the deeper the fish are during the summer. The water normally is a little cooler down deep. Keep in mind certain lakes develop thermoclines and

Summer can offer both exciting and challenging bass fishing. Successful tactics will vary a great deal across the country, mostly according to water clarity.

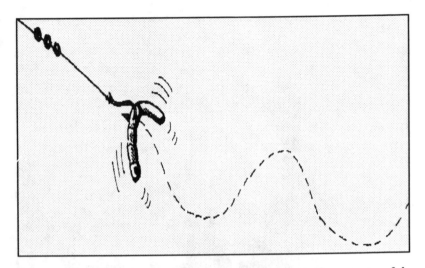

The rhythm method of plastic worm fishing is especially effective for post-spawn fish. It utilizes a special rig consisting of a light wire hook run through the center of a small plastic worm, normally 6-inches in length and fairly hard. The hook is left exposed. The line is normally 8 pound test with split shot above the worm. This is a finesse method of swimming the tiny worm in rhythmic twitches.

below these fish have oxygen problems. Bass will often bunch up right above this level. Say this level is 35 feet. Fish where this depth intersects a productive piece of structure. An example would be a tapered point along a creek channel at the 35 feet zone. Work with big plastic worms and even a jig with a motion trailer.

Clear water lakes normally offer the best fishing at night during the summer. An example would be lakes like Table Rock and Bull Shoals in Missouri and Arkansas. These lakes normally offer good topwater action early and late in the day (low light periods) around main lake points and along bluffs and deeper areas.

On some off-color (dirty and stained water) areas of certain lakes like Truman in Missouri, fish stay shallow during the summer. Fish get in the heavy cover along creek channel edges and can be caught with spinnerbaits, buzzbaits, and flipping and pitching jigs and worms. Wherever you fish keep in mind that water clarity plays a big part in determining where the fish will be. Dirty water lakes normally are not good night fishing lakes.

Summertime also offers schooling fish activity on certain lakes as schools of bass follow, chase, or ambush roaming schools of shad and other forage.

Lakes like Eufaula in Alabama also can be great when they generate water and the fish set up and feed along the main river channel. Some great catches can be made by paying attention to generation schedules. This moving water can really get some summertime hogs biting. Plastic worms fished Texas and Carolina style get the nod as being the most productive but some of the new deep diving cranks can also account for some awesome catches.

Keep in mind that water color is your big key during the summer period and use things like generation current and low light to your advantage. This is the time of year you have to constantly be thinking to be consistent. Analyze your situation and make adjustments accordingly.

FALL

Fall is the season that more and more people are realizing can be fantastic. Summer boat traffic subsides and some of the best fishing of the year takes place.

The bass move back onto the flats and into the creeks and start tearing up the bait as the water cools down. Lots of fish suspend in tree tops and around boat docks to ambush bait schools. Fantastic buzzbait and spinnerbait fishing can be had along with good action on Spots, Cordell's Ratt'l Spot, Bomber Ratl RRR, and other shad colored crankbaits.

During this time of the year bass move up tree lines and fence lines. They also migrate up the creeks and this can be one of the strongest patterns going. Put your boat in a creek channel and crank the edges, bouncing baits off of stumps, etc., until you locate the stretches and depths that are holding the fish. This was a pattern that was evident at West Point Lake in Georgia several years ago. Tom Mann, Jr. won the tournament fishing a jig through the stumps along a creek. Rick Clunn was second fishing a crankbait along a creek in another section of the lake.

If you happen to get fall rains and a rise in water, lots of fish will head for the banks so pay attention to the water level. This happened at the BASS Buggs Island, Virginia tournament in 1989--all the top places came from shallow, heavy-cover flipping and spinnerbaiting. This tournament would probably have been won cranking structure and creek channels if not for the rise.

Fall can be fun and exciting. It can also bring some great topwater action. A big key to fall fishing is fish where the majority of the food supply is and pay attention to creeks and creek channels.

Individual Water Analysis

Analyzing the lake you are fishing is important for success. No two lakes are alike and realizing each lakes features and potentials can greatly influence how you fare.

First, what type of lake are you going to fish? Is it a highland or lowland type of reservoir? A highland reservoir will be deeper and probably clearer. It could certainly call for lighter line and maybe even finesse techniques. A lowland reservoir would be more shallow, more fertile, and probably have more water color. Power baits would more than likely play a bigger part.

If you are going to a river, determine if it is tidal influenced. That can tell you a lot of what to expect and how to prepare to fish it. The more information you can gather about the place you are going to fish, the better you can prepare yourself to meet the challenges it will offer.

Keep files on lakes that you fish or are planning on fishing and keep all magazine articles and other information that could be helpful in the future. Also keep detailed notes of your trips so you can refer back in future years. This is very important if you fish tournaments. It can give you an edge. The mind has ways of blending lakes together, but your notes will keep you straight.

Some anglers use tape recorders and record their angling days for the future. As I travel home from tournaments, I dictate and my wife takes notes. I go over each day (practice and tournament) in detail listing everything that might be a key on a future trip.

Some anglers make calls to area marinas seeking current fishing conditions, patterns, and lake conditions. This can be good but you must be careful about chasing patterns that are no longer current. You are always better developing your own patterns as conditions dictate. Self confidence breeds success.

Something I have made a habit of doing when going to a strange lake is to fly the lake. You can learn more in 2 hours in the air than you can in 2 days in a boat. Carry a map up with you along with a notebook and pen. Mark spots of interest on your map with a number and then write corresponding notes in your notebook. This is a quick and neat way to keep track of what you see. Keep track of water color changes, water bird activity, areas which might indicate more fertile areas or bait fish. Actually look for schools of bait fish. Keep track of cover options available and mark them. This way you know all the options the lake has to offer before you make your first cast. Then when you do get on the water and get something working, you know where to duplicate it.

In tournament fishing, pre-flying a lake can be a true edge although I have had some wild flights that made me question this method of analyzing a body of water. Typical of this is a flight I made over Lake Mead in Nevada. Not more than a few minutes into the flight oil started spraying all over the windshield. There aren't many places you can set a plane down, the terrain is just too awesome, but the pilot finally managed to land on a little, narrow dirt road. He got out, wiped the oil off the windshield, said they just overfilled it, took back off, and started flying over the Grand Canyon. There we were with no place to land. I didn't learn a thing on that trip, because my eyes were glued to the oil pressure gauge.

Map Study Made Easy
(Eliminating Unproductive Water)

This actually goes hand in hand with analyzing a lake. It is one of the most important things you can do to make yourself a better fisherman on a given body of water. Map study can be very exciting and rewarding if done correctly.

First, find the best maps. Cheap, simple maps are fine for navigational purposes but seldom have the details you need to determine bass holding areas. Try to find good contour maps with the contour lines as close together as possible. This

Make notes of all conditions while fishing and keep a log book. This will help in future trips regardless of whether you are tournament angling or fishing just for fun.

helps in showing subtle changes. Topographical, hydrographical, and navagational maps are the best.

Once you have your hands on a good map it goes back to analyzing the lake. What do you already know about it? Does it have hydrilla or milfoil? If yes, how deep does it grow? What time of the year will you be fishing the lake? Keep in mind the seasonal patterns and you are on your way to easy map study.

If it is spring the majority of the fish should be 10 feet and shallower. Get a highlight pen and shade everything from the 10 feet contour line to the shore. This should show all the flats and potential spawning areas. Also highlight any humps or ridges that are 10 feet or shallower that the fish might be using. You've just eliminated a lot of water.

You might be hunting summertime fish that are in the

23

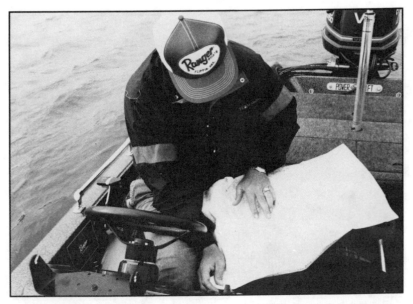

Map study before your fishing trip can eliminate a lot of unproductive water. Use a highlighter pen to mark key areas that look the most productive.

25 to 35 foot range. Do the same thing. Highlight this zone and then pick out the most productive looking areas. This system allows you to focus on what is pertinent about the map at the given time or season you are fishing. This can especially be helpful in allowing you to identify areas before you fly a lake.

Time spent with a map almost always pays big rewards. It helped me win my first BASS Sam Rayburn tournament. I had highlighted the shallow areas feeling that bass would be in the pre-spawn stage. I also noted and further highlighted all

Tip--When you highlight a map you'll be amazed at how many subtle areas you'll find that you would never have found just by studying the map.

depressions and creek channels that ran through these flat shallow areas. When a big cold front hit during practice, my maps showed the obvious places for the fish to move to. I flipped the willows next to these ditches and won the tournament. Don't look at map study as boring or a waste of time. Look at it as one of the easiest ways you can gain an edge over fellow anglers and the bass itself.

Electronics in Finding Fish

Electronics play a very important part in being a complete, versatile fisherman. At times you can get by without them, but they will almost always make you more proficient. The most important piece of electronic equipment for finding bass is the locator. It is your underwater eyes and should

Electronics are extremely important tools for any bass angler.

I utilize a flasher on the bow of my boat with the transducer installed on my trolling motor so I know exactly what is under the bow of the boat.

constantly be feeding you information to help catch more fish.

I grew up with flashers and still use them, but the trend the last few years has been in the LCD type units. These are fine and for lots of people easier to interpret than a flasher.

My boat is currently set up with a flasher up front that I can monitor while running the trolling motor. The transducer is mounted on the head of the trolling motor so I know exactly what is under the bow of the boat. On the console I have an in-dash flasher for navigating and a CVR (color video recorder) for more detailed information. These transducers are mounted in the rear sump area.

No matter how your boat is set up, pay attention to your electronics and use them to your advantage. In shallow water they can be a definite aid in showing you the subtle changes that

An in-dash flasher is mounted in the console with the transducer mounted in the sump area. This provides instant information for navigation and fast fish finding.

hold fish. In deep water fishing they are a must to keep you in the productive zone. I once saw Randy Fite pull up on a flooded road bed and start spooning it. Suddenly he spotted a fish suspended up off the bottom, brought his spoon up to the proper depth, and caught the fish. You can't do this if you haven't paid close attention to your electronics.

In the fall of the year, on lakes like Table Rock, I have done extremely well using electronics to find the schools of shad out on the big gravel points that run off the main river channels. I can stay over a school of shad and jig grubs or tube baits over and through them. I have caught some very large Kentucky Spotted Bass with this technique. I usually fish these baits on 6 pound test Stren line in 25 to 50 feet of water depending on the forage location. I always try to keep the

A CVR or color video recorder on my console provides more fully detailed information. The transducer is mounted in the sump area.

sensitivity on my sonar turned up so I don't miss any activity between me and the bottom.

If you are not sure what your unit is telling you, go out with someone who is good with one and brace yourself for a learning experience. Humminbird as well as most of the other electronic companies also have manuals available to help you learn to use your units properly. Just spend some time on the water with them, and you'll be amazed.

The flashers, LCR's, CVR's, charts, graphs, are all very important for finding fish, as well as fish holding areas, so pay your dues and learn to use them properly. There are, however, other electronic devices that can also help you find and catch more bass.

A temperature gauge is a must, especially for early

spring fishing. By knowing the temperature you know what patterns should be working and what lures to try. Finding a pocket with just a few degrees warmer water can make the difference between a successful day and no bites at all. You will also be surprised how much the water surface temperature can vary as you move from place to place around a lake.

A personal weakness of mine is that I leave other electronic devices such as pH and color monitors alone. I have always felt common sense and experience would be more reliable. If you believe in them, however, and they help you catch more fish, then by all means use them. Who knows, maybe someone will convince me that they'll help me catch more fish. None of us know all the answers so we must remain open-minded and willing to listen in order to continue to learn.

Use your electronics as aids to help you eliminate water and find fish but don't get so carried away with all of it that you actually don't have time to fish.

Using Currents and Tides to Your Advantage

You will hate them or love them depending on what you know about them. Currents and tides can definitely affect the areas bass are using and can be assets to you in finding and catching them.

First you need to determine if you are dealing with man-made or natural current. We touched on man-made current earlier with summer generation on lakes. Bass feed and become more active when water is being released creating a current in the lake. Certain lakes, like Eufaula in Alabama and West Point in Georgia, are famous for the bass feeding according to the generation schedules and water releases. It boils down to timing. You can be sitting on the best point in the lake getting no bites and suddenly they start pulling water and you load the boat. Find out the generation schedules, if you can, and it will help your fishing on these types of lakes. An example would be if they are going to start generating at noon, I would probably fish shallow, more active fish until noon and then pull out and take advantage of the fish that are conditioned to feed with the current.

Natural current takes place on the rivers, creeks, and upper ends of most lakes and reservoirs. Rather than constantly fighting the current, bass set up on ambush points out of the current and take advantage of bait being swept by. Understanding how they position can eliminate a lot of water for you and make the fish holding spots pretty obvious.

Finding bass consistently is a process of elimination and duplication. Eliminate patterns and waters that are not productive and duplicate places and patterns that produce. If you have a mile stretch of river that is bare and then suddenly you have a couple of stumps or a little cut, it is pretty obvious a bass is probably laying there out of the current. You may go another mile and find the same situation and catch some more. You are then on your way to a very successful day.

This is one thing I really do not like about fishing tournaments on a river. Unfortunately, all the good spots are easy to recognize. In order to win you have to be fortunate enough to find one of those subtle, off-the-wall spots that everyone overlooks. Paul Elias and Jack Chancellor both did an excellent job of this in their Bassmaster Classic wins. They found areas that really did not look good but had everything these current fish needed. A tough job for sure but one that can be very rewarding.

Fishing tidal current is really no different except that timing is extremely critical. Tidal fish move a lot but are very predictable. If you catch them off a spot, pay attention to the time and tide level. The next day if you are there when the same situation (tide level) takes place, you should catch them again. Pay lots of attention when you catch tide-water bass and get a tide chart. Catching these bass can become very easy if you get your timing down on all the spots you locate. Some spots will be good on high tide, some on low tide, and others at certain stages in between. It's your job to determine when a spot is best and then duplicate your timing on it in the future.

I have had some of my best tidal fishing within two hours either side of low tide. When I was pre-fish practicing for the 1989 Bassmaster Classic on the James River in Virginia, I saw just how important timing can be. I fished a wooden structure at the mouth of one of the creeks thoroughly and never had a bite. I went back into the creek and fished around for about 45 minutes without any action. As I was coming back out of the creek, I noticed that the wooden structure seemed to have more current running by it. The tide was starting to come back in and the current had indeed picked up greatly. I stopped and fished this same spot and immediately caught about 15 pounds of bass. Timing is number one when it comes to fishing tide water bass.

Combine what you know about where bass like to sit out of the current, find these spots, be there on time, and load the boat. Current and tide truly can make finding bass easier.

This whole section has been geared at finding bass--the most important part of successful fishing. Anybody can catch them if they are around enough of them, but nobody can catch them if they are not where the bass are. Refine your skills at finding bass consistently and you can compete with anyone or any condition.

Understanding the effects of weather on movements and patterns of bass is extremely important for consistent productivity.

Chapter 2

USING AND UNDERSTANDING WEATHER

How Bass Respond to Stable Weather

Stable weather is to bass fishing what rain is to making your grass grow. It definitely makes for more productivity. First, however, it is best to totally understand what is taking place in the fishing world in regards to weather.

Weather is one of the single most important things to consider when it comes to bass fishing. If you understand how bass relate to the weather and its influences, they are a lot easier to figure out how to catch.

Normally the bite gets better each day the weather is stable until some system comes in and rocks the boat. Then the process starts all over again until the next system hits. It stands to reason that if the weather has been stable all week leading up to a week-end fishing trip or tournament, the fishing should be excellent.

Lots of patterns could be working and fish should be aggressive. If you are not getting bites, you better try another area. Stable weather also normally allows you to fish faster and cover more water in your search for bass because you know they should be in a positive feeding mode.

If the water temperature is warm enough, the topwater bite should be good. You, however, have lots of options available for catching bass. This is the weather condition or scenario that most fishermen prefer. The bass's mood remains constant day after day so once you establish something, it's pretty reliable. Personally in a tournament, I prefer changing weather conditions because I know it will change the bass and lots of the existing patterns. If I understand these changes better than the other contestants, my odds of winning go up. That is why it is so important to keep track of the weather and its changes.

I try to keep track of the weather in tournament locations for a couple of weeks before I actually go there. I fished a tournament a few years ago on West Point Lake in Georgia in the fall that was a perfect example of what the weather can do. Leading up to the tournament the weather was very stable and I thought there might be a possibility of enough fish shallow for some type of pattern. I knew the majority of fish would be caught along the creek channels and on deeper structure but that is also where the majority of the contestants would be. I thought that if I could get any type of shallow water bite going, I might be able to win since I would have it basically to myself. During pre-practice I was able to establish one of the strongest Lunker Lure buzzbait bites I have ever seen. I just put the trolling motor on high 24 and started down flat gravel and clay banks chucking and winding. About every quarter mile or so I'd have a three to eight pound bass jump all over the bait. This pattern held up in every area I tried. I was sure I could easily weigh 30 plus pounds a day during the tournament.

The night before the tournament started a big cold front rolled in and destroyed this pattern. It dropped the surface temperature a few degrees and the fish totally left the buzz bait bite. I caught a few in the same areas on spinnerbaits but nothing compared to what it would have been if the weather had stayed stable. The second day after the front the weather improved and the surface temperature started to pick up a little. By the afternoon of the third and last tournament day, the weather was getting stable, the bait were back up, and some bass were again feeding a little more aggressively.

It was on this last afternoon that I witnessed one of the best examples of true sportsmanship I have ever seen. I had one bank I'd run every day and then leave and go fish other spots. At the end of this bank was a long point that Charlie Campbell had fished every day. We honored each others spots and stayed on our own areas the first two days and both caught a few fish. The last day I decided to save that bank until late in the day because I felt the bass would be more aggressive then. Charlie and Larry Nixon were paired together the last day and were working Charlie's point when a large bass started blowing shad up in a little flat pocket on my bank. Knowing that all they had to do was move 100 yards and they could surely catch that fish, they elected not to. They figured since I had not run the bank yet there was a chance that I might still fish it. I came rolling in on the far end and they immediately came down and told me about the bass and to be sure and work the little pocket good. They then got back on Charlie's point and went back to fishing and watching as I worked towards the pocket. On my first cast through it with the Lunker Lure I caught the fish. It blew up on the bait and was a very welcome 5 1/2 pounds to my stringer. It was also the difference between a nice check and no check. This shows you the extreme sportsmanship and class that both Charlie and Larry possess.

They are both good friends but I am sure they would have acted the same regardless of who was fishing that bank. The tournament trail is full of countless stories like this and that is part of what makes it and the people that operate in this manner so special. Hopefully more people can learn to fish with the same standards as the true "pro's". Whether you are tournament fishing or just out bassing, courtesy goes a long way toward making our sport more enjoyable. I am sure no one likes someone to pull in front of them on a bank so don't do it to the next guy.

Just remember if the weather is stable, the fishing should be good. Fish faster and try more patterns.

How Bass Respond to Cold Fronts

The cold front is probably the most used excuse there is for failure to catch bass. It has destroyed more patterns and crushed more dreams than all other weather situations combined. It separates out the good fishermen.

I am not sure scientifically what happens to the bass during a cold front. From a fishing standpoint, it is easier to explain. As an example, let's say a big bass lives by a bush. Under stable weather conditions its strike zone may be several feet around that bush, depending on water clarity and sky conditions. The bass is aggressive and will chase the bait. This makes lots of lures and techniques possible fish catchers. Even the poor casters catch fish under these conditions. When the cold front hits, this strike zone shrinks. The worse the front, the smaller the strike zone. Under bad cold fronts, the bass will barely move at all to get a bait. A bass that was aggressive the day before suddenly is not biting. Instead of laying beside the bush, the bass is now in the middle of the bush and more than likely in the thickest part and not willing to come out and grab normal offerings. This is where the techniques of flipping and pitching can be so effective. We devote a chapter to these techniques later in the book. What is important now is to

During cold fronts bass tend to move deeper or tighter into cover, reducing the strike zone and requiring more precise lure presentation.

realize that the bass has changed its mood because of a weather change. It has also changed its location because of a weather change. You can see why paying attention to the weather and learning how it affects bass is so important.

What a front does to bass depends a great deal on the severity of the cold front and where bass were holding before the front hit. If bass were positioned on main lake points, they may just back out into deeper water and suspend, and these are indeed very hard fish to catch. If they were on relatively bare banks or flats, they may pull to the nearest drop or creek channel. If they were on the edge of a creek channel, they will probably drop down into it. The examples go on and on.

The one situation and key that has won lots of money for me is when bass are shallow, a front hits, and cover is nearby. Rather than go deep, they simply bury up in the heaviest cover they can find. Just like a covey of quail that were out feeding in a field during good weather will head for the brushpiles and bury up when a snowstorm hits.

Now, if parts of this heavy cover have deep water next to them, they should be better than the rest. Also, say there are fifty bushes on a flat and all are in about the same depth except ten that are a little bit deeper. After the front those ten will more than likely hold more bass than the other forty combined. These are just examples, but hopefully they will get your mind working in the right direction.

In clear water situations you can normally get more action after a cold front by down sizing your lures. If you were catching bass on a five-inch grub before the front, a three-inch grub will work better after the front. Irregardless of the water color, for consistent success you must slow down and be more precise with your presentations after a cold front. Repeated casts or flips to certain areas may be required to generate a strike. Analyze how severe the front is you are dealing with and where the fish were before it hit. Pay attention to how much the water temperature drops and determine what options the bass had and where they moved.

I actually look forward to cold fronts in tournaments because they eliminate so many patterns and frustrate so many competitors. If you know the options left for the bass you can use the cold front to your advantage and catch some giant stringers of bass. The key is to fish slow.

Rising and Falling Water Levels

This is a night-and-day situation. It can be either good or bad, but it always affects bass and their movements. If you are headed to the lake or a tournament this is one of the first things you should check. If you are going to be there for several days, poke a stick into the lakes edge by the ramp. That way you know from day to day what the lake is doing and can adjust accordingly.

If you are just going fishing and have a choice between a rising or high and a falling or low lake, normally the rising lake will offer the best fishing. Rising water has helped me to a lot more high finishes in tournaments than dropping water ever has. Keep in mind that the fish are normally doing the same thing as the water. Everything of course is relative to where the fish were before the change in water level occurred.

If the fish were on secondary points and the lake came up, they would probably move to the backs of pockets. If they were in the backs of pockets and the lake started to drop they would probably pull to the secondary points. This is an example of what can happen. When I give examples, I am referring to what the majority of the bass are likely to do. One thing for sure in bass fishing is that there are no sure things.

Some bass always go against the normal "flow." Call them flukes or stragglers or whatever, but keep in mind that not all bass are doing the same thing. In most instances, however, rising water usually means the fish will be fairly shallow and pretty aggressive (depending on the weather). If the lake gets up and floods into grass and bushes, look out. Some of the best fishing you can ever have takes place when this happens.

As an example, in 1985 I participated in a US Bass Tournament on Table Rock and the lake was high, about five feet above normal pool. The water was up into the grass and bushes. I won the tournament and set an all time record by catching a ten fish limit that weighed 48 pounds. Since that

A stick poked into the waters edge, or other markers can be used to note rising, falling or stable water levels.

time the record may have been broken, but what was unique about the tournament was the fact that Table Rock Lake normally doesn't have that pattern,but was a perfect example of how the fish can absolutely go crazy when a lake gets up. The first day I went up one arm of the lake and caught a limit of spinnerbait fish, then went to a bush and caught a 6 pounder off it with a jig. Then I went to a cove where I had previously caught a lot of keeper male fish to give my partner a chance to finish catching his limit. I pulled into the cove, he caught his limit and I caught a few more. The fish seemed aggressive in that cove, but we never caught any really big fish.

I came in third place in the first day and figured I should go to the same cove right off the bat on the second day, get a limit of the smaller fish, then move on up to a spot where I had caught a nine pounder in practice. I pulled into the cove and on the first bush I came to I caught a six pounder. The big fish had all of a sudden decided to move up into the flooded bushes of my little-fish cove. I moved down the bank a little further, put a spinnerbait into some flooded grass, quickly caught 4 more just keeper fish, the moved a bit further to a laying down log and caught another six pounder. I decided to stick around and fish a bit longer and pitched a jig into a bush and caught a seven pounder. Naturally I fished a little more, pitched a jig under some overhanging limbs and caught an 8 and a half pounder.

Needless to say, there was no way I'd leave that cove the rest of the day. That day I weighed in a limit of five fish that weighted 29 pounds and easily won the tournament. It was one day of fishing I'll never forget and an example of just how great a lake can be when the conditions are right. If you have a choice of going to a lake that is high or one that is normal, or dropping, it doesn't take long to make up my mind. I'll go to the one that's rising or high. We run into this situation quite a bit and almost always the fishing is great. In fact, rising or high water has accounted for several tournament victories for me.

Flipping and pitching the newly flooded cover can be great, while spinnerbaiting and buzzbaiting the weeds can also be fantastic. If the rising water has dirtied up the lake, that in itself will move more fish shallow. If the lake has gotten just plain muddy, you might need to look for the clearer or stained sections. This is another situation where flying the lake can be such an advantage. It will show you all the water color options and you can then decide what degree of dirty water you want to fish. If everything is really muddy, usually the farther back in the flooded grass, the better the water quality. The grass strains the silt and the bass move back in it.

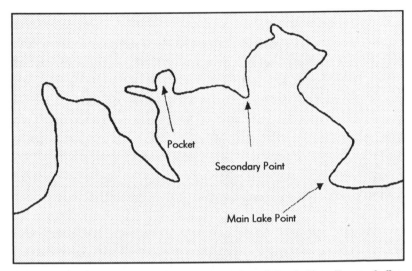

Bass move with rising and falling water levels. With rising levels they will move shallow or into the backs of pockets. With falling water they move to the points. If they are in the pockets, they will usually move to the secondary points first.

When water rises and floods above normal pool line, behind willows, bushes, and in green vegetation, bass fishing can be fantastic with buzzbaits and spinnerbaits.

The worst bite is normally in cold muddy water. If the whole lake is muddy, find the areas with the warmest water temperature. This is why anglers immediately start hunting for off color water during tournaments.

On Lake of the Ozarks which has hundreds of boat docks, fish hang around the docks for cover. With a rise, they often just move to the back side of the walkway supports or into shallower water. Rising water definitely moves fish.

Falling water can also be used to your advantage to find fish although lots of times they are not as aggressive as when it is rising. Keep in mind that as the water drops back so do the fish. Take an area with a bunch of flooded grass. As the water drops, fish pull to the edge of the grass and hold there until it drops so much it forces them to leave and then they head to the areas they were before the water came up. It's the same with flooded bushes and trees. If a few are deeper, those are the ones the bass will be forced to pull out to. Normally on dropping water, the point bushes are where the action is.

Falling water can really help concentrate bass on certain objects. This was the case in 1987 when I won the "BASS Angler of the Year" title along with winning the Super Invitational on Kentucky/Barkley Lakes on the Kentucky/Tennessee border. The lakes had been high and were dropping. The fish had pulled to the few deep-point bushes left and were using the current from the pulling water to ambush bait on these points. In the flats where the cover was too shallow if you could find a piece of brush or an isolated log laying out in front of these now too-shallow areas, it would have a good fish or two on it. Most of the contestants were fishing the drops because they felt all the fish had already pulled out, but what were left were big, aggressive, and very predictable. You just had to find the right places and make lots of stops, covering lots of water.

43

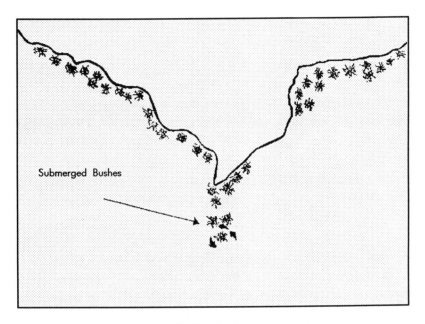

Submerged Bushes

Once water starts dropping bass will follow the drop moving to deeper water structure, often concentrating bass in point bushes.

I ended up winning by a large margin even after breaking a prop shaft the last day and losing most of the day to down time.

   The dropping water had allowed me to concentrate on key spots and win. I have found schools of good shallow water fish at other times and thought I could win only to have it get too shallow. As the water dropped the fish would move off and I never could relocate them in time. There are no guarantees. Just use good judgment, bass are in places for a reason. They will stay as shallow as they can even on dropping water if there is forage, shad, cover, or whatever to hold them there.

   Rising and falling water level is just one more piece to the puzzle that helps you find fish. It gives you another way to help stack the odds in your favor. Another important factor is location and mood of the bass.

Wind (Friend or Foe)

Just like fluctuating water, the wind can help you or hurt you. I have seen days when the wind was a plus and days when it destroyed the fishing. Normally in bass fishing the wind is an advantage unless it gets out of hand. Lots of fishermen never capitalize on the wind because they always fish the protected areas. Admittedly these areas can be easier for boat control and casting efficiency, but very seldom are the bass as active there except during the cold water months. Then the protected areas can be more productive and any wind can hurt.

The clearer the water you are fishing, the more important the wind is. Wind breaks up the surface and makes the fish more aggressive. I have seen times when you could not get a bite and then the wind came up and the fish went crazy. At certain times the wind can become part of your game plan. Some of the summer tournaments I have fished on Lake Mead in Nevada really illustrate this factor. I'd work deep points early until the wind got up later in the day and then go to the windy banks and work topwaters and spinnerbaits.

I have also seen the wind get too strong and make boat control and fishing almost impossible. At times the wind can prohibit you from getting to productive areas. It also can quickly turn nonproductive areas into bonanzas.

The wind enabled me to win the 1985 BASS tournament on Chickamunga Lake in Tennessee. I fished large coves on the lower end the first two days and was sitting in 10th place going into the last day. The nine in front of me looked like a who's who of bass fishing. At noon the last day I had yet to catch

> **Tip--A spinnerbait on a windy bank is one consistent pattern that has saved many a fishless day.**

Wind can be friend or foe. It can sometimes turn bass on or sometimes it can cause miserable fishing and unsafe boating.

my first fish and I knew that if I was to have any chance to win I would have to gamble and make a move. The wind had come up strong, blowing 25 to 35 mph. I began thinking about a large group of fish I had found up the river on my chart recorder. They were suspended beside a ridge, laying out in the main river under a huge school of bait. I had spent a lot of time in practice trying to catch them to no avail. I thought the wind would move the bait in on the shallow ridge and the fish below them would follow. I still didn't even know for sure if they were bass. My partner agreed to make the long, rough ride up the river knowing the gamble.

The wind was so strong by the time we got there that about all we could do was blow down the ridge throwing crankbaits. I kept the boat in the deeper water and made casts up on the ridge. I was able to catch three bass that weighed seventeen pounds on the first two passes. We then had to navigate the rough water back in but made it just in time. I ended up winning by a couple of pounds thanks to the wind and knowing how it can affect bass.

At times this also means not being afraid to finish last. I sure don't recommend running in windy water that you or your boat are not capable of handling. No bass is worth a life or an injury. Use good judgment on the water and also when you buy a boat. When you buy a boat keep in mind where you are going to be fishing and if it is suitable for the adverse conditions you might encounter. My first boat was a 12 foot john boat which was fine for fishing the little protected back-water areas in the watershed lakes around my home. However, I realized that in order to have more freedom chasing bass and patterns all over the lakes and on larger waters, I needed to move up in boat quality and size. My wife and I worked hard and bought our first brand new Ranger bass boat.

I have run a Ranger since and know that whatever conditions I encounter, my boat is the last thing I need to worry about. That is a very comfortable feeling when you fish for a living or if you are out fishing with your family. Safety on the water is very important so keep that in mind when you go boat buying and buy quality. A boat is no place to cut corners.

I have seen the wind dirty up an area because of wave action and ruin the fishing, but most of the time when it dirties up an area a little bit it is a good place to check out and throw a spinnerbait. The wind will also beat weeds like hydrilla and milfoil loose and stack and mat them in places. Pay attention to wind directions during storms then on the following day check wind blown mats, they may have fish under them.

A little tournament trick I employ is to use the wind to get fishing areas to myself. Lots of times in practice you can trailer to areas that contestants can not get to because of rough water. Because they did not practice there, they probably won't go looking come tournament time. If the wind lays somewhat you can run to these productive areas and virtually have them to yourself.

I was able to do this in the first BASS tournament that I won on Sam Rayburn in Texas. The wind blew hard all throughout practice and I trailered up the lake to an area and found some good bass. By the time the rest of the field found these fish during the tournament, I already had a good lead.

The wind can also create some good current in places and get the bass feeding. This happens a lot on lakes like Okeechobee where the wind can funnel water through breaks in the rim channel and also through vegetation openings.

Obviously you can tell I like the wind and the advantages it can give you. If you start to look at wind as a helper rather than a problem, it will put more fish in the boat.

The Moon and Its Part (Solunar Tables)

This is an area that I wish I knew more about. I really don't think if I knew more it would change my style of fishing any, but then again it might. Whether you believe in the different solunar tables or not, keep in mind that the moon and sun and the different moon phases certainly play a part in fish and wildlife activity. I go fishing as often as I can, as early as I can, and stay as late as I can. Therefore it makes no difference to me when the best bite is going to be. I am going to stay in the areas I feel I can get the most bites according to the current conditions.

The one moon phase I pay attention to is the full moon during the spawning months. Over the years we have observed a definite increase in spawning activity and movement into spawning type areas during the full moon. The moon also plays the all important role with tides and their changes.

Anything that gives you more confidence in catching bass is good. If the solunar tables and being in a certain spot at a certain time makes you fish better, then you will have more success.

Rising and Falling Water Temperatures

We have talked some about this but it is important to add a little more. As you monitor all your different weather conditions to help you find bass, keep in mind what these changing conditions are doing to the water temperature. We know that a severe cold front is going to drop the water temperature and the bite will not be as good. We know that on a cloudy day the water temperature will not rise as much as if it were sunny. We know that the wind can pile up warmer surface temperatures in certain areas. We know a lot about what causes the rises and falls in water temperatures, but we still have to react correctly to these changes.

A good example of how critical adjusting to these changes can be was apparent fairly early in my career. Back in the early 80's Jimmy Crisp won $100,000 in a US Bass Tournament on Table Rock. During that tournament I was on a bunch of fish way up the White River and they were spinnerbait and jig fish. The lake was high and the majority of the fish were in the heavy cover. We were going through a lot of weather changes--it would cloud up, then get sunny. I was really working at figuring how to catch them. I'd work a spinnerbait when it was cloudy, but when it became sunny I had to get into the cover with a jig. When the tournament started the water temperature was fairly cold and I was throwing a light jig with a big pork frog. It had a pretty slow fall and kept the bait in front of them a bit longer. It seemed to trigger the fish and is probably the reason I did so well in the first part of the tournament. It was an elimination tournament and eliminated part of the contestants in the first part of the tournament. In the final day there were only five of us fishing for the $100,000.

As the week progressed we had extremely warm weather and the water temperature just kept warming. Everything became more active, the metabolism of the whole ecosystem was increasing to the point that I was no longer using the correct presentation. I needed to move my baits faster and I didn't pick up on this until the last day. By that time the temperature had risen 8 or 9 degrees, I was still using a fairly slow falling bait and was having a hard time getting bites. Larry Nixon was fishing the same general area of the lake and he was throwing a heavy jig on a tip he had picked up from Tommy Martin, that the most strikes were coming on a heavy jig down

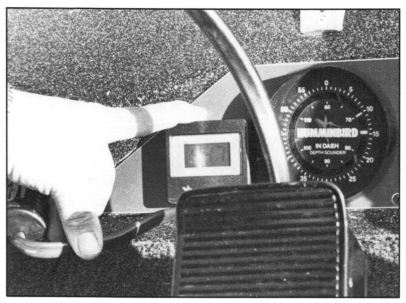

Varying water temperatures can also greatly affect bass movements and locations. Regular temperature readings are important.

in the bushes. It was more of a reflex strike. Nixon, fishing the faster falling jig put together an incredible stringer that weighed 20 plus pounds and I thought he had it won, but the one angler that took it a step further was Jimmy Crisp. He figured the water had warmed enough the fish should be moving out of the bushes, so why put a bait inside the bushes. He went with a big Rapala type bait, jerking it by the willow trees, and the fish would run all the way out and grab it. He ended up catching a five fish limit that I believe weighed about 25 pounds and ended the tournament with $100,000.

As you can see from this story it doesn't take much time or temperature change to alter the mood of the bass. In this case it was simple, a little warmer water and a rise in the fish metabolism. By paying attention to water temperature you know which lures and techniques will or can work. The easiest way to look at water temperature in regards to bass fishing is the colder the water, the slower you must fish. A drop in temperature means you need to slow down from what you had been doing. The warmer the water, the faster you can fish because everything has speeded up due to an increased metabolism rate. A rise in temperature normally means you need to speed up the fall or retrieve of your lures. Temperature can give you the clues then you need to learn what techniques and lures to use and when. This is just another key ingredient to using the weather to find fish. I have caught bass through the ice and I've caught them in water in the 90's.

How Bass Relate to Sky Conditions and Changes (Storms, etc.)

This is the weather factor that can change in minutes and has to be constantly monitored. I always try to find a complete weather report for the day I am going to be on the water along with the forecast for the whole week. This helps give me an idea of what patterns are likely to be good and which ones could change.

An example would be a clear lake where a topwater bite is good on cloudy days and bad on clear sunny days. A fish is loose to cover when cloudy, tight when sunny. A fish is also shallow when cloudy, deeper when sunny. You can be fishing a worm under sunny conditions when all of a sudden some clouds roll up. The best bite might now be on a topwater or spinnerbait. I have also had times when I was catching good fish on a cloudy day, and bang the sun came out and I had to switch patterns. At times it just means you need to switch colors. You may be worm fishing on a cloudy day and a dark

A bright sunny day is my personal preference during tournaments, especially if some type of heavy cover exists.

colored worm is working well. Suddenly the sun pops out and the fish are not biting as well. You may simply need a different color, maybe a blue or red or something lighter. Normally the darker the sky conditions, the darker the bait. I have had a lot of success with a black Lunker Lure buzzbait on dark, cloudy days and during early and late low-light periods. However, I have never done well with this color under bright conditions.

I personally like sunny days during a tournament, especially if some type of cover exists. Normally, under bright conditions the fish get tighter to cover and you know exactly where they are. Under cloudy conditions they often seem to be more free of cover and more roaming. Keep in mind that sky conditions at times also affect algae blooms and bait fish activities which in turn affect bass movements.

Cold water fish normally bite better under sunny skies and warm water fish under cloudy skies. Clear water fish bite better under cloudy skies and dirty water fish bite better under clear skies. There is no magic formula but simple things to keep in mind as you continually analyze the changing conditions around you.

Storms are a different type of stimulant to the bass. I have seen greatly increased feeding activity right before a storm moves in. Learn to read the weather and don't take chances on getting caught out in it. Lightening is very dangerous, especially when you are on the water. If you do get caught, seek shelter accordingly. Lightening and thunder seem to put a damper on biting fish. At times it seems to drive them deeper or tighter to cover. Rain on the other hand is a plus. It breaks the surface up and seems to turn the bass on. I heard Charlie Campbell say one time that if you can't catch fish during the rain, you best quit. Before you take up golf, however, keep in mind that you still have to be where there are fish.

Some of the biggest bass I have caught have been on rainy days. It seems like they are a little more susceptible. Shallow, clear water fish are also easier to catch during the rain. For some reason snow also has the same effect. Obviously the action will be somewhat more subdued because of the cooler water temperatures. Keep in mind that lots of times you can increase your action once some type of precipitation starts and also you may have to change your techniques to match this weather change.

An example would be catching the fish on a jig and frog when suddenly it starts raining and they get on a good spinnerbait bite. Stay alert and adjust. Lots of time these are subtle changes.

Fog is another condition that can increase your number

A compass is an extremely important piece of equipment on any boat; enables you to navigate in fog, darkness, or on unknown lakes.

of bites, but it also can create navigational problems. Fog to me is the most dangerous boating condition. Definitely use common sense and never run a boat on plane through a fog bank. All major tournaments get held up until the fog lifts because of the danger. I also run a compass on my Ranger boat just in case fog sets in during the day.

I hope this section on using the weather combined with the one on finding fish helps put you in more productive water. I know that if you get conditioned to paying attention to all this, it will definitely help.

Understanding the different types of cover, and how bass utilize each under varying conditions, can mean the difference in a poor or a successful fishing day.

Chapter 3

COVER PATTERNS AND OPPORTUNITIES

Flooded Willow Trees and Bushes

This, without a doubt, is my favorite type of cover to fish. Flooded willow trees and buck bushes are some of the best bass magnets. Lakes like Sam Rayburn in Texas, Grand Lake in Oklahoma, Buggs Island in Virginia, and others are notorious for their willow tree fisheries when the water rises. You still need to learn to capitalize effectively even though you know the fish are in this cover.

Determine the pattern-within-the-pattern. In a mixture of willow trees and bushes some days they will all be in the bushes and other days all in the willow trees. At other times they will all be on the dead willows, or on the live bushy willows, and the same with the bushes.

Bass can also get particular about the size of the tree or bush. At times they are on the edge and other times in the middle--at times suspended and other times on the bottom.

Bass have quite a few location options with the type of cover, so pay a lot of attention to where you are getting your bites and then simply start duplicating your successful areas. This enables you to fish faster, more thoroughly, and therefore cover more water. This is very important in a tournament situation because time is so critical. Why waste half your time making casts to the sunny side when all your bites are coming from the shady side or vice versa.

Where and how the trees and bushes are positioned can also make a difference. At times cover next to ditches and deeper water are the best spots. Other times the point piece of cover or the cover in the back of a pocket or the isolated cover is best. Pay attention and it gets easier.

One of the most exciting experiences I have had fishing willow trees happened years ago when I was still in Nebraska fishing small tournaments in the Blue Valley Bass Club. We had a June tournament on Merrit Reservoir, a sandhills lake. I found the fish in the willows and figured they would come out of them and eat a topwater bait. They were hitting a white Devils Horse really good. The water was clear and I'd throw the bait quite a ways past the trees and work it back in short jerks. If you brought it all the way in this way you would swear no fish at all were in the trees. However, if you stopped it beside the trees and just let it sit, in a few seconds you would see a bass swim out from the tree, stop about a foot below and behind the bait, then just watch it. When you gave the bait a little twitch, they exploded on it so fast it scared you. Talk about fun, that's about as good as it gets. My partner and I ended up first and second and far out-distanced the other contestants.

There are lots of lures and techniques that work around this type of cover. The flipping and pitching methods are excellent with jigs and worms and so is spinnerbaiting and buzzing the bushes. In clear water, skipping a tube bait up tight on the light line can get a lot of strikes. The time of year, weather, and existing conditions will tell you which baits work best in this type of cover. Just keep in mind that if you get on a lake and find flooded willows and bushes, you just may have the best fishing of your life.

Flooded timber, willow trees, and bushes are some of my favorite types of cover. It is important, however, to determine the most productive at the time.

Stump Rows and Fence Lines

These are very consistent fish holders and also very obvious. I like to fish submerged stump rows along old river channels. They can be dynamite but hard for a lot of fishermen to find. The shallow, obvious ones on a lot of lakes get fished pretty heavily but still produce to a certain extent. As you run to the upper end of a reservoir, the submerged river edge stumps suddenly begin to show up. Normally there is a two or three mile zone where the stumps are still pretty hard to spot on the upper end that I like to key on, especially if the area has a lot of current. The fish will hold on the down side of the stumps, out of the current. You can run a crankbait by them or flip a jig and pitch right above them and hop it by and get your arm broke. The submerged stumps can be dynamite fished with a crankbait or a jig and frog. Keep in mind that if you see a few stumps on a point or on a ridge, they probably run on out into the lake.

Fence lines are the same. By observing the shore and what is up in the fields, you can detect fence lines running into the lake. The hard-to-find ones are going to be very consistent bass magnets while the obvious ones will get fished hard. Fence lines are one of the easiest pieces of cover to fish and they can be fished in a variety of ways.

If a fence line has current or a good wind blowing, I love to crankbait it. If not, pitching worms and jigs can be very effective. If you have a place where two fence lines meet or where a ditch or some deep water crosses or gets close to the fence lines, pay attention.

A couple of tips for actually working fence lines that can make them more productive--If the wind is blowing, put the boat on the downwind side and throw into the wind. This

Any location where two migration routes, such as a fence line and a ditch, cross are prime bass-holding spots.

makes casting a little harder but also makes your bait appear a lot more natural to the bass. I also try to keep the boat on the shady side of the fence line so I can fish the shaded area, not throw my shadow on the fish and risk spooking them. If you have ever watched bass in shallow water react when a bird flies over and casts a shadow, you know why this is important.

Water birds are natural feeders and enemies of the bass when they are young and this fear of moving shadows at times can send them running. I have had, however, bass on some of the clear desert lakes actually pull under my boat and swim along in the shade or shadow that it was creating.

Inobvious Banks and Cover Situations

Nowadays inobvious and subtle banks and cover situations are more of a key to good catches, especially if you are on a heavily fished lake or in a major tournament. Fishermen are very educated these days and know what most of the textbook spots look like. We will get into this in detail in the tournament strategies section. For now we are interested in the spot rather than the reason.

Areas that look like they would not hold bass are worth looking at very closely and you can't do that running down the lake at 60 mph. You need to idle down some of these banks and pay attention to the isolated cover or break changes. Some of my best spots most people would never dream of fishing.

Map study can help show you a lot of these subtle spots or at least what should be the most productive parts of a non-productive area. Unfortunately, this can also mean going against what the majority of the fish are doing. Keep in mind, however, that what looks bad might be good. Try to find reasons why a place can hold fish rather than why it shouldn't and you are on your way to learning how to find the inobvious spot.

The Hard Stuff (Rip-Rap, Bluffs, Rocks & Gravel)

Not all lakes have all of these cover options but almost all of them have at least one. Even a lowland mud and clay bottom lake usually has rip-rap around bridges or dam facings. This is a good place to start and rip-rap is a favorite of mine.

Rip-rap is a very obvious cover structure, but seems to always hold bass. Sometimes the most obvious gets left alone. Rip-rap fish can be caught in a lot of ways but crankbaiting at a 45 degree angle with my casts is a favorite. Use crawdad colored cranks early in the year when the bass are chasing crawdads and shad colored the rest of the year when shad are the main target.

Rip-rap often wedges jigs. Hold rod tight, pull line taunt, and snap bow and arrow style to unwedge jig.

A jig and frog can also be great, cast in the same manner as a crankbait. Keep in mind, however, that jigs can get hung pretty easy in rip-rap because they wedge. Try to swim them a little more than you normally would and you won't get hung on rip-rap nearly as much. One thing you can do when you do get hung is the old bow and arrow routine with your rod. It will work a lot of the time to free your baits.

Early in the year, when the water is cold, concentrate on the rip-rap and other rocks that are getting lots of sun exposure. In warmer water, key on the shady banks.

If you live in the Ozarks, where I do, you will love fishing bluffs. There are a lot of lakes all over the country that provide good bluff fishing opportunities. If you have Kentucky bass in your lake, there is a good chance they will use the bluffs for part

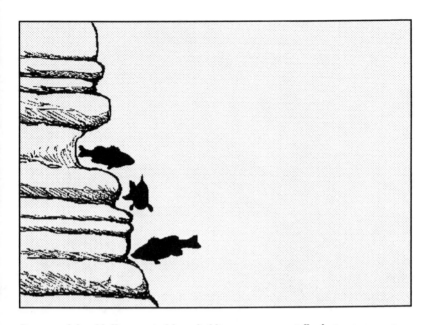

On many lakes bluffs are good bass-holding areas, especially during temperature extremes of really hot or cold weather.

of the year. Bluffs seem to be at their best during the temperature extremes. When it is real cold a lot of fish winter along the bluffs and when it is real hot they pull along the bluffs for shade and deeper, cooler water. Keep in mind, however, that not all bluffs necessarily have deep water against them in all places. Lots of times you can find one of these bluffs or walls (as they are called on the desert lakes out west) and it will have a rock slide or two where parts of it have slid into the lake or river. These offer something different and can be excellent holding spots for bass. Deep cranking slides with perch or bluegill pattern crankbaits can be very good in the warmer months.

In clear water these same areas and even the walls can be good fished with 6 and 8 pound test line throwing 4-inch worms and tube type baits.

Lots of fish suspend along bluff walls so you need to figure out the depth your strikes are coming from and keep your bait in that area as much as you can. Bluffs are always better fishing opportunities in clear water. Usually in stained or dirty water bass use shallower structure. Look for irregular places in the bluffs--cracks, ledges, slides, points, pockets, all can be good. Usually a bluff is a place where the main river channel makes a swing at the shore. The spot where it hits and the spot where it leaves the bluff are the key spots. At times the fish will stack up on the ends of these bluffs during the fall and can be caught fishing deep with a jig and frog or a jigging spoon.

Another fall pattern, especially for Kentucky bass, is taking a big bladed spinnerbait and burning it parallel to the bluffs. A big Colorado blade is best with a white or chartreuse skirt. Keep the boat tight to the bluff and go down it reeling the spinnerbait as fast as you can.

Chunk rock and broken rock banks are fished almost like rip-rap. Keep in mind that they normally hold lots of crawfish and this in turn helps attract the bass. My favorite time for fishing the chunk rock type banks is late winter and early spring and my favorite technique is casting a jig and frog on 10 to 17 pound test Stren. Some huge pre-spawn fish can be found bunched up on these broken rock banks so really key on them early in the year. Crawdad colored crankbaits can also be good worked along them in a stop-and-go fashion. If the water is clear a jerkbait like the Spoonbill Rebel can be good along the chunk rock, especially when the water is still cold.

Gravel is normally an area that bass use only for a limited amount of time. Gravel is at its best during the spawning season. The more protected it is, the better it will be. A favorite of mine is pea gravel pockets next to chunk rock banks. Bass will often hold on the break between the two. This can

Chunk rock banks can also hold a lot of bass especially in late winter and early spring when bass are feeding on crawfish.

also hold true where a bluff turns to chunk rock. The gravel banks are at their best if they have some other type of cover to help hold the fish. On gravel banks bass love the bottom makeup but like the security of some type of cover. These are the banks you hunt for during spawning season and also the banks you can work with a number of techniques. We talked about the spawning cycle and what baits worked best earlier, so just keep in mind that the fish do use these banks and figure the technique and bait to match the conditions.

Keep in mind that there are endless examples of hard cover or different types of rock habitat. Also remember that a combination of any two types of cover is always better than a single type of cover by itself. The key area will also always be where the two types of cover join.

Boat Docks, Piers, and Seawalls

Lakes like Sidney Lanier in Georgia, Lake of the Ozarks, and others, come to mind when you think of boat docks. Boat docks are "bass condominiums" and come in all forms. There are numerous keys to figuring out which docks are best. Let's look at some examples.

First keep in mind the type of shore and bottom make up where the dock is located. A dock on a pea gravel bank will be great around spawning season but could be fishless the rest of the year. By the same token a dock on the main lake would not be as good as one in a pocket when the fish are on this type of bank. During the warmer months, and especially the fall, the docks with the wind blowing on them will be better. Docks with pilings are normally better than floating docks.

At times fish will be on the deep end and at times on the shallow back side. The back side is a favorite pattern of mine early in the year because most fishermen don't bother. They simply fish the front and sides and go on. Even the walkway supports can be key spots. Try to pattern the dock fish. At times they may be on the docks that have a ladder hanging down in the water. At times around boat lifts. I like to key on the older docks because they build up algae on the supports and pilings and this in turn attracts bait fish and they attract bass. Normally the older docks also have a better chance of having some type of manmade structure or brush on the bottom under them. If you spot a dock with spot lights, rod holders, chairs, or anything that might indicate people crappie fish, check it over. More than likely it has a brush pile under it which will also hold some bass.

Gary Klein won a BASS tournament on Sidney Lanier in Georgia shaking a small worm on light line down in the brush

Boat docks and other man-made structures can provide extremely good bass fishing on some lakes if you pattern the dock fish.

piles under docks in the clear water of that lake. Most were Kentuckies, but largemouth use the docks equally as well.

A Lunker Lure clattering down the edge of a dock, or a Zara Spook worked alongside have both caught lots of bass for me. So has tossing a grub on light line into the boat slip and letting it free fall in the shade for bass suspended under the dock. I have done well pitching a jig and frog around and behind docks and also swimming it by them just under the styrofoam flotation. This can be deadly in the fall. Docks are bass magnets so check them out but remember some are better than others--pay attention to what is holding the bass on certain ones.

Piers are almost as good as docks but do not offer as much shade. I have had excellent pier fishing on some of the rivers such as the James in Virginia. Here heavy current runs by the piers because of the tidal fluctuation. I fish these situations almost like a fence line, staying down wind or down current, throwing past, and bringing my lure into the cover naturally. Crankbaits are really a favorite for pier fishing. If you catch one bass off a pier there is a good chance for a whole school. On rivers I like the piers best in the summer periods. On lakes I like them best in the spring.

Seawalls are great if they also have current running by them. Then if they have a break or corner bass will stack up and use them for ambush spots. Shallower seawalls are great early in the year, especially in protected areas like canals. In Florida I have caught some huge spawning bass around shallow seawalls working floating lizards in slow erratic jerks. If its springtime or there is a current, check out the seawalls.

Manmade structures can be almost anything from a boat ramp to a partially sunken boat. One time I caught several nice bass during a Bassmaster Classic on the Arkansas River out of and around an old sunken car. On river systems you often run into sunken boats and barges and they can be great. The Hudson River in New York has provided some excellent fishing around sunken barges on more than one occasion.

The boat ramp pattern can be great if you live on a lake that has lots of launching areas and private ramps. Fish will use the edges and ends of the ramps for shade and ambush points. Kentucky bass can really get on this pattern in the spring and be caught with the Zara Spook. Metal boat rails that run into the water can be great in late winter and early spring as they draw and hold heat which pulls the bass to them. I have seen bass on Grand Lake fall to a jig from this pattern. I once found a swim slide beside a boat dock that had a metal four way support. This was on my home lake and over the years I have probably taken twenty bass over 5 pounds out from under this metal slide. Keep in mind that not all the good bass spots are textbook pure examples.

Brush Pile Building

Brush pile building is one of the best ways I know to concentrate fish, as well as make a good spot a great one. It is truly amazing how fast bass will move into a new piece of cover. First, always make sure it is legal in your state or body of water to put in brush. In some places it is illegal because of fear of navigational hazard. Check first rather than be sorry.

Another nice part is that if you do it right, you will be the only one that knows the location. Those bare pea gravel banks we talked about earlier are excellent choices for brush piles. I have even made artificial fence lines with brush piles so that the bass have a choice of depth. You can even suspend brush by tying styrofoam to part of it so that it offers another opportunity for the fish.

A great way to enhance a dock is to weight a tree and let it hang off the dock rather than go all the way to the bottom. I like my brush (mainly cedars) to be dead before I sink them. Green cedars in my opinion give off a toxin and can ruin an area for a while. With other types of trees it is not a problem. Green willows seem to draw fish as fast as anything but they don't last as long. You can imagine all the hot spots you could make if you took a day or two and you and a buddy built a few spots.

In my opinion if everybody did this it would improve the habitat on every lake to the extent that the overall fishery would improve. I know the bass club I formerly belonged to (Blue Valley Bass Club of Seward, NE) works with the game commission every winter on brushing projects on area lakes.

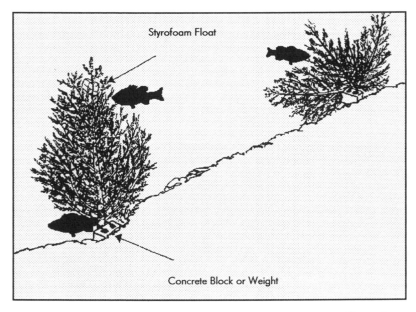

Styrofoam Float

Concrete Block or Weight

Building brush piles, where legal and where they pose no navigational hazard, is a great way of attracting and concentrating bass.

Everyone benefits from projects like this and clubs that take the time, money, and effort to do this are truly appreciated. If you put in trees and brush, do it correctly. Take the time to anchor it properly so it will not become a hazard and so that you get several years of fishing.

I have put brush piles in 2 to 30 feet of water and done well. Some piles always hold fish and some never do. I have been fooled a few times and placed some piles that never did attract fish. One time I had a big tournament coming up on a lake and figured I could concentrate a bunch of fish at about the 5 to 15 foot zone with brush piles. A friend and I put in 115 brush piles. We worked from dawn to dark for two days. Come tournament time some fronts had rolled through and all (the majority) of the bass were still deep. The tournament was won between 35 and 50 feet. I never had a bite from any of the brush piles I put in. It just was not right for that depth. The next time I go I may catch two bass out of every brush pile. Keep in mind one good pile in the right place is better than ten piles randomly placed. These also benefit species like crappie and bluegill.

Cattails, Reeds, and Bulrushes

I have seen some fantastic stringers of bass come out of this type of cover. I had a friend flip one over 13 pounds out of a patch one day. This is great cover for big bass. Cattails grow shallower and are not as consistent as the deeper growing bulrushes. When fishing cover of this type the keys are often the same--points, pockets, breaks, anything different seems to be the productive spots time and time again. It seems like you can go down the straight stretches for a long time without getting strikes.

Another thing I hunt for are the thick or matted spots. These are especially good after cold fronts. Another tip is the darker colored patches are normally a little deeper or nearer to deep water. Flipping and pitching are great techniques around this type of vegetation. One practice day on Okeechobee I caught two bass in the 10 pound range in less than an hour flipping a worm to the bulrush points. Pitching a spinnerbait way back in bulrushes can also be very productive. At times, where you do not have a defined line of cover, you can quietly sneak or blow through the area flipping or pitching to the isolated clumps. This is brutal cover so gear up with heavy line and hang on. Also keep an eye peeled for movement or shaking of the stems. On numerous occasions I have seen reeds shake, made a pitch to the spot, and caught a bass. Also

> **Tip--Slimy fish scents are great when fishing stem type vegetation with a worm. The slicker you can keep the worm, the easier it will slide through the cover.**

when you flip or pitch into the cover, if the cover shakes by your bait, get ready. More than likely that bass already has your bait.

Also pay special attention to any piece of wood that may be mixed in with this type of vegetation. Remember any combination of cover is better than one by itself. The same is true with vegetation. Okeechobee is a good example with areas of mixed grasses and isolated pencil reeds. During the spawning months the fish relate to these pencil reeds so work them over with spinnerbaits, topwaters, and worms. One lonely pencil reed in a field of pepper grass can hold a big bass.

Hydrilla, Milfoil, Lily Pads, and Pepper Grass

This is another love'em or hate'em section. Some of these grasses or weeds are very controversial and have really been the center of attention in certain areas. Let's start with hydrilla and milfoil which have been the object of intensive eradication programs in some areas.

A major example is the TVA chain of lakes. Lakes like Chickamauga and Guntersville have become great fisheries thanks to the invasion of milfoil and hydrilla. However, they are constantly being sprayed by the powers-to-be in an effort to control or eliminate them. If they succeed in eliminating these weeds, they will also eliminate the quality fishery. Hopefully a happy compromise can be figured out. The introduction of grass carp is a scary option being employed, but that is a story in itself. As a fisherman all we need to know is that bass love this cover, so let's explore ways to catch bass from it.

73

Lily pads have been a traditional bass fishing hot spot that today still produce some of the best in heavy-cover bass fishing.

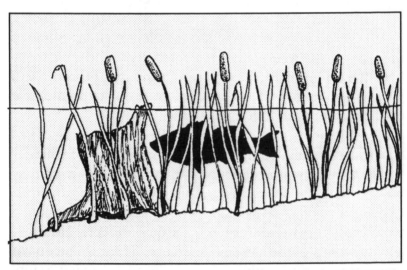

Bulrushes, cattails, and other aquatic vegetation offer extremely good bass-holding spots. When combined with wood such as stumps or lay downs, they are fantastic.

This vegetation normally grows in a certain depth band. Say from 5 to 15 or 20 feet depending on water clarity. The inside of this band will be the key during the spawning months and the outside edge of this band will be the key during the warmer and winter months.

Naturally where unique structure gets tight to this edge is a plus. An example is a creek channel that swings up against the weed line. Early in the year while the grass is still way below the surface, you can slow roll big spinnerbaits and run baits like a Ratt'l Spot over and through it. Once the grass gets to the surface and mats you can pitch jigs or worms down through the holes and almost vertically jig the bass into biting.

Bass relate to the edges but at times move way back into the vegetation. When the fish are way down deep in the hydrilla on lakes like Sam Rayburn and Toledo Bend, you need jigs up to 1 ounce to get down to where they live. Isolated clumps in shallow or deep water are almost always a bonanza. Flying over a lake can help you spot some of these as can good map study by showing the humps and ridges where the grasses could be growing.

Another early season technique I've had good success with around milfoil is a jerk bait pattern. Jerking a bait down by clumps and edges of the grass can definitely bring out the bass. The Bomber Long A is my favorite for this. The Spoonbill Rebel can be great worked in the same stop-and-go jerking motion on the deep edges of the grass lines.

Lily pads are associated with bass more than any other type of vegetation. They are good bass magnets but not what they are cracked up to be. For one thing they grow on soft mucky bottoms which are not a bass favorite but at certain times of the year bass do get in them. Florida is an example of an area where bass spend a lot of time in the pads during the colder months. In some areas they even use the massive lily pad root systems to spawn on. I won $41,000 one time in Florida by pitching a worm down into the pad roots and shaking it. Heavy line is a necessity fishing the pad roots because they are extremely tough. If you get a big bass on and can't clear him of the cover, go to him rather than pull on him. You'll land a lot more fish if you keep cool and dig them out.

A pattern I really hate to talk about because hardly anyone does it is crankbaiting the pads. I love to take a Bomber 6A or 7A and crank it through the pads. You'll be surprised how you can work the bait through without getting hung up. I have caught several 7 and 8 pound bass with this pattern not only on the edges of the pads, but by running it right through the pads as well. The firetiger color is normally my favorite but you might experiment depending on existing conditions.

Spoons are great for pads as well as the other grasses. One type of cover where they really excel is in pepper grass. Take a 1/2 ounce Johnson or Rebel Arrow Head Spoon, put a trailer on it, and hang on. I'll talk more about the baits and how to rig them later, but for now keep in mind this is a great option for the tough-to-fish grasses.

One thing about pepper grass flats is that they are hard to run a trolling motor in. You definitely need some type of weedless prop and a powerful motor. I use a 12-24 Evinrude high thrust trolling motor which is the quietest, most weedless, and powerful motor I have found. When fishing these flats I like to blow across them with the wind, working my cast at 45 degree angles from the boat until I find a school of fish. It is best to drop a marker as all these areas look alike and getting back in the right area once you have blown by can be tough.

Some of the grasses and vegetation can be very hard to work and boat movement can be hard. Keep in mind, however,

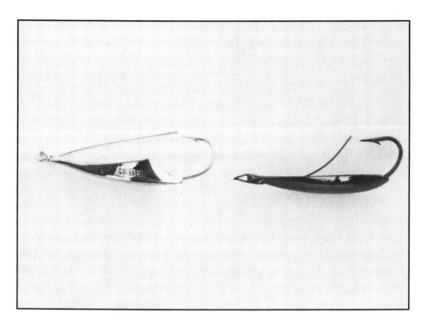

A wide variety of spoons can be used on vegetation such as hydrilla, milfoil, lily pads, pepper grass, etc.

that all the work can be very rewarding because grass and bass do go together.

Ledges, Structure Breaks, Creek Channels, and Humps

Years ago most people fished the bank. Then a couple of anglers won tournaments fishing out in the middle of the lake and it became the in thing to do. These days most good anglers are capable of running the banks and visible cover patterns along with fishing the hidden structure. Examples are endless so use your imagination.

Ledges or structure breaks can be the primary holding

spots for the majority of the bass, most of the time, on most lakes. They do not have to be picture perfect either. At times just a 1 to 2 foot change can hold a bunch of fish. Naturally a break with any additional type of cover like brush or stumps can make it even better. Shallow ledges and breaks out from spawning areas can be great for pre-spawn bass and again for post spawn bass so hunt for this possibility. Carolina rigged worms or lizards can be great for fishing these subtle drops. If you have trouble fishing the correct zone get a half dozen markers and drop one every 50 to 100 yards then work the break. When you locate the fish, triangulate the spot so you can easily find it again. Going down structure breaks with crankbaits is a good way to locate fish. Then you can slow down and fish more efficiently with other lures.

Creek channels in my opinion almost always have a population of bass using them. The problem is locating the creek channels. Some creek channels run for miles so take some short cuts. In the spring and fall the back one-third of the creek should be more productive. During the peak heat of summer and coldest part of winter, the front or lake side third should be the best. The other third is the buffer zone and depending on conditions can go either way.

A little tip about marking a honey hole especially in a tournament situation where it is important to be able to find it in a hurry. If you leave a regular marker buoy on the spot someone will probably find it, so take a small, two-inch square of styrofoam, a piece of monofilament, and an old sparkplug. I even paint this brown to make it hard to spot unless you are looking for it. You can even take a stick or piece of wood that looks natural and use it as your float. I also do this on key spots in grass flats to mark the location of schools of fish.

Definitely pick up your markers the last day of the

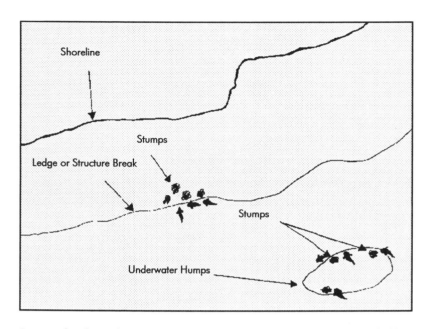

Structure breaks or elevation changes such as ledges, humps, etc., are major holding spots for bass on almost all lakes.

tournament for environmental reasons. There is enough trash and discards on our waters without adding to them.

I also like my transducer for my front locator glassed in up front on the head of my trolling motor. It allows me to stay more precisely on the edge of the creek channel or break.

Every time I think of fishing humps I think about a dreadful day in the fog down on Toledo Bend. I have however had some days on humps that were very good to me. I remember one time on Truman Reservoir years ago when I was guiding a client and I got into the bass big time on a hump. We were tied to a tree throwing to a bare spot on the hump with plastic worms. Every cast we had a strike and the bass were running from 2 1/2 to 4 1/2 pounds. We did this for about an hour and it never let up. It is hard telling how many fish were in that school. We were releasing every fish and even those were not scaring the school off. I think it was absolutely the biggest school of fish that I have ever set up on, and all while I was tied to one tree. Then the nightmare started. The man I was guiding decided he wanted to go back in a creek and have me show him how to flip for a while. I figured he had lost his mind and tried to talk him into staying put. He said he needed to rest from catching all those bass and that way he could learn while he was resting. Later we could come back and catch some more. I tried to tell him he could rest while I continued to jerk on them but of course he didn't buy that.

Eventually I quit and showed him how to flip and we even caught a few fish doing it. After about an hour and a half he was ready to go back to the hump. We went back and tied up to the same tree and never had another bite. The school had moved off. I will never know how large that school was but I bet that man never wants to leave another school of biting bass. I have dreams about getting into that school again only now they probably weigh over 7 pounds.

Another time I was pre-fishing for a tournament on Truman and working a shallow hump along a creek channel. I caught three bass over 8 pounds on consecutive pitches with a jig and frog. Then I took it away from one in the 10 pound class that came up and rolled with the bait. I shook off several more strikes before leaving. It was a sure enough school of giants that I wish I had worked over because I never have contacted this school again. Sometime I will and if it's during a tournament, every record will be broken.

Humps are good in all seasons depending on their depth. Naturally shallow humps will be more consistent in the spring and fall with the deeper humps the key in the summer and winter. Lots of techniques work, depending on depth, but

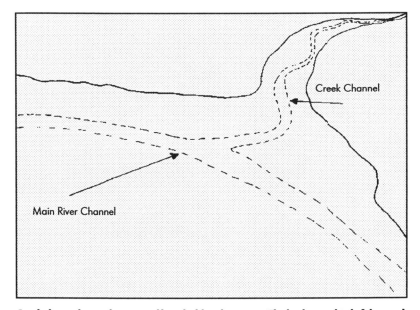

Creek channels are always good bass holding locations. The back one-third of the creek is best in spring and fall while the front third or lake side is best during the heat of summer and the cold of winter.

keep in mind the Carolina rig, an excellent way to cover the water in a hurry. A crankbait that will get down and dig the top of a hump can get results too.

Lay Down Logs and Log Jams

Laying logs first of all are fabulous fish holders. I love fishing shallow heavy cover and laying logs are a true favorite. For one thing you can use several productive techniques for fishing them. I love pitching jigs or worms around them, but bringing a crankbait alongside them can also catch some giants. A lot of times I'll crank heavy logs with 30 pound test Stren Magnathin in order to control the big fish when they bite.

81

Lay-down logs provide some of the best in big bass cover. Any number of tactics and lures can be used on them.

    The spinnerbait ranks as the number one laying log bait because you can do so many things with it. Don't be afraid to let it flutter down or bump the log on occasion. The big key with laying logs is their location. Logs on pea gravel banks are great in the spring. Logs on flats are fantastic post-spawn and fall spots. Logs on steeper chunk rock or channel banks can be great in the summer or winter period. It is really hard for me to pass up a lay down log.

    Jim Bitter almost won the 1989 Classic by making repeated casts to logs back in creeks that had current running by them. Persistence at times pays off well on the isolated logs.

    I'll never forget one laying down log at the 1985 Bassmaster Classic on the Arkansas River. Most of the fish were coming out of the backwater areas and I figured if I could find

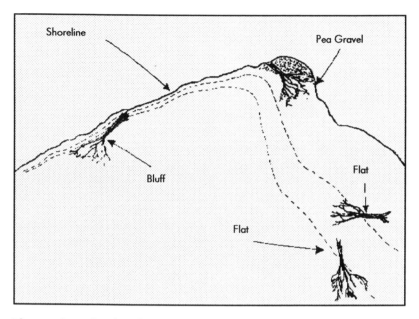

The main key to lay-down logs is their location. Logs on pea gravel banks are great in spring, logs on flats are good during the fall, logs on chunk rock or bluffs are great in summer or winter.

a backwater area no one else was getting to, I'd do good. I pulled into the mouth of a little bitty creek you could go probably a quarter of a mile back in. Then I came to a giant log that was laying across the creek and kept me from going back in to what looked on the map like it opened up into a couple of backwater lakes. It looked like there simply was no way you could get around, under, or over this log. It was huge! It stuck three feet above the water, but I thought if I could get at just the right angle, I could jump a boat over the top of it.

The first day of practice when I found the area I had a rather large press observer with me and figured that simply wasn't what I needed to be jumping across a log with. I needed someone light but with some strength in case we got stuck.

83

That night I told my wife I had drawn an outdoor writer named Louie Stout, who looked like just the right guy to jump the log with. I drew a map and told her that in case we got across the log and couldn't get back out, here's where she needed to send help to come and get us. We were going to be back in the boonies in the Arkansas River and there's no way we were going to walk out with the snakes and everything.

We idled up to the log, I trimmed the engine up so I could get the nose of the boat up high and got the nose started up on top of the log. I just kept giving it a little more gas. Louie looked at me like I was crazy. And I guess I was. I just kept on giving it a little more gas and the boat would run about half way up on the log, then slide back into the creek. I told Louie when I got it going to the point it was up on the log he needed to run to the front of the boat and move the weight forward so we would drop over on the other side and slide off the log. We did everything right and sure enough it dropped over the log on the other side.

The only problem was the boat landed on top of a stump on the opposite side. That left us with the bow of the boat sitting on a stump and the back of the boat sitting on a log. It was just like putting it on a trailer. None of the boat was sitting in the water and the prop was about a foot away from the water. We were anchored. You couldn't even rock the boat. Finally, we took the Boat Rein on the front of the boat, made a lasso out of it, lassoed another stump up ahead and I got out on the log. Between Louie pulling on the rope and me rocking the boat on the log we finally got it to slide off.

Sure enough, the further up the creek we got, it opened up into a beautiful lake which was unfortunately absolutely loaded with carp. We never got one single bite! All that effort to get back into a place to win the Classic, and everything was perfect, except no bass lived there.

The next problem was getting back out. I told Louie we would get out one way or another. There might not, however, be a motor on the back of the boat when we finished. We nosed the boat back up the log, gave it gas, and simply shot over the top of the log. We didn't do any damage to either the boat or motor, which says a lot for how Ranger boats are built. It was unbelievable what we put the boat through that day and you couldn't see a mark on it. It was a hilarious situation, and I regret to this day we didn't get out on the bank and take a picture of the boat sitting high and dry!

Log jams can hold bunches of fish and can be great flipping bonanzas. Another time I was down on the Alabama River practicing with a friend for an upcoming Classic tournament. As we were running down the river we saw a couple of pockets that had floating logs and weeds all piled up into a big mat. I thought some fish might have moved in under the debris pile so we pulled in and started flipping around and sure enough caught three or four pretty decent fish. I thought there was a good chance those fish might hole up in that spot. All we needed to do was punch a few holes down through the matted cover then I'd have a bunch of holes to drop my worms and jigs down through. Part of it was so solid you couldn't even get through but I got out a push pole and a paddle and we began trying to make holes. I had driven the boat right up on top of the log mat and we were poking around trying to make holes.

Suddenly my friend lost his balance and the next thing I knew all I could see was two tennis shoes sticking up through the log jam--the rest of him was beneath the water. Suddenly his feet disappeared, then finally his head poked up through the debris, covered with weeds, spiders, and all kinds of crawly critters. Of course he couldn't sink because all the debris kept

85

him from going to the bottom. It took me forever to get all 280 pounds of him back in the boat. While he was trying to dry off and clean up, I told him I appreciated his help in poking holes in the log jam, but I really didn't want one big enough to run a buzzbait through.

That kind of area, with a combination of log jams, weeds, and matted debris, can hold a bunch of bass any place and any time of the year. We often catch bass out from under such jams, called 'sawdust piles', in cold water (below 41 degrees) on Truman Reservoir. This is primarily due to the fact the wood warms from the sunlight and warms the water below. The best tactic to use for these fish is to drop a heavy jig down through the 'sawdust.'

Suspended Bass in Trees (Nightmare or Bonanza)

For most people suspended fish are indeed a nightmare. Let me give you a few pointers that might help.

First, on lakes with lots of timber, forget the timber is there! Look at your maps and find areas where bass should be even without the timber. Then check the spot and use the timber as an added plus. An example would be the trees on the outside bend of a creek channel in the middle of a major bay, or on a flat next to a deep water channel.

Next figure out what depth the bass are holding. Are your bites coming near the top or in the mid range? On cloudy days bass are normally suspended closer to the surface and can be caught with spinnerbaits, buzzbaits, and Zara Spooks. On bright days they suspend deeper in the trees and dropping a big worm, jig and frog, or jigging spoon may be the ticket. A huge, 13-inch worm produces good catches when bass are suspended in timber on Truman. Pay attention to the depth the trees are

Although some consider suspended fish a nightmare, when suspended in trees they are much easier to catch. The key is to locate areas and depth where bass would be even without the presence of timber. Timber is just an added plus.

located in where you are getting bites. Even though your strikes are coming at say the 10 foot level, they may only come from the 25 foot deep trees.

The type of tree is also important. Bass may all be in the cedars, oaks, thorn trees, or on just any big hardwood. Under different circumstances bass forage may be attracted to specific types of trees. The main key to getting good at catching these fish is paying attention to all the subtle things these suspended bass are relating to. At times on lakes like Sidney Lanier you will be looking at submerged trees on a locator or chart recorder so it becomes even more of a challenge. It can be very rewarding, however, as I've caught some good Kentucky bass by spooning these deep trees for suspended bass.

Fishing Points and Soil Changes

Points are very popular in the fishing world for lots of species. They are good feeding areas and offer a variety of depths. Normally we divide points into two groups; main lake points and secondary points.

Main lake points will be best in winter and summer and secondary points in spring and fall. Techniques are endless depending on the slope of the point and the conditions. Early in the year a favorite tournament pattern of mine is cranking points with a crawdad colored bait. You can work a bunch of points in a day and usually do fairly well. This is a great back-up pattern. If nothing else is working you can almost always go to the points and catch a few fish, sometimes even load the boat.

Map study can show you the inobvious points that should be better on heavily fished lakes. We could spend a lot of time talking about points but they are so basic that most people fish them pretty well. The only mistake I normally see is that in the summer people do not fish points as deep as they should. Pay attention to the bottom make up of the points you get bites on and duplicate this feature if you can. At times the points that have heavy wind blowing in or across them can be dynamite.

Soil changes are one of the subtle patterns because they normally go unnoticed and unfished. Let me give you a few examples of what I look for--sheer rock turning to broken rock, broken rock turning to gravel, gravel turning to sand, sand turning to mud, and mud turning to clay. Any change or edge can stop and hold fish. Check these spots. They only take a few seconds and can lead to some strong patterns. Just the color of the soil can be a preference for the fish.

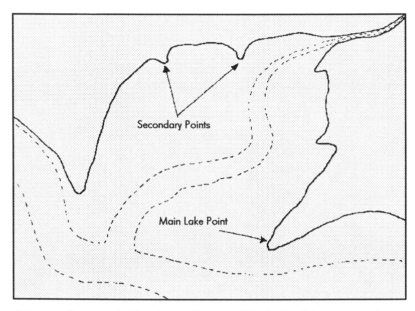

Points are always good although usually heavily fished. Main lake points are best in winter and summer, secondary points in spring and fall.

I hope this section has given you some added ideas and options as far as places to look for bass. There are a lot of different types of patterns and cover opportunities on most bodies of water. Just match the cover to the correct time of year or seasonal pattern, adjust it to the existing weather situation, and make adjustments as needed.

Choosing the correct lure to meet the varying situations is an extremely important factor in successful bass fishing. Plano Tackle Stacker helps organize lures.

Chapter 4

LURE PRESENTATION AND TECHNIQUES

Crankbaits

Out-of-the package crankbaits are about the best fish locators on the market but also the lowest fish catchers. Hopefully I can highlight a few things that will help put more fish in the boat for you when you use crankbaits.

There are countless models, sizes, and colors available. This is one lure category where a lot of anglers get caught up in lure collecting. You really need to look at crankbaits as tools that will do certain jobs. Get some that will do different things. Get baits that run effectively at different depths. A few super shallow, shallow, mid-depth, and deep divers. Then have a few color selections to meet existing water and sky conditions. Also different sizes can be important under certain conditions.

The super shallow divers are often overlooked and yet one of the best fish catching baits. With them you are throwing a crankbait in places where bass are used to seeing spinner-baits, buzzbaits, worms, and jigs. You are giving bass a new look. The key is being willing to throw the bait where you might not get it back. This is hard for lots of people and understand-able with the cost of baits. It is also the reason you need to develop confidence in a few baits and then carry duplicates.

Once you learn what you can do with certain baits,

Crankbaits are the best fish locators and are available in countless models, sizes, and colors. You will need a selection including super shallow, shallow, mid-depth, and deep diving.

you'll also find you won't lose as many. You'll be able to throw a crankbait into a brush pile and finesse it all the way through without getting hung up. When you run the bait down into the bushes and it starts to hang, just give it a little slack, let it float back up, and then move it forward into the next underwater limb and do the same thing. This stop, back-up-and-go technique in brush piles is deadly on big bass and it is amazing how many places you can work a bait through.

A buoyant crankbait is a must for this technique. Most buoyant cranks float up and slightly backward when you give them slack line. That is why you can work them through these spots. Keep this in mind in all your crankbait fishing and you won't lose as many baits. If you keep pulling, they will hang up.

If they get wedged, the old bow and arrow snap will usually free them. If you do have to break off, the bait will often float up.

These super shallow and shallow baits are also good in lily pad fields. You can actually work them through the stems without getting hung up.

With hard bottoms, I like to have the bait digging in and bumping along. With a soft or silty bottom, I like to have the bait running up off the bottom. Bass will aggressively strike a bait on a hard bottom but try and pin it from on top in a silty or soft bottom. This causes you to have bad hookups and miss or lose more fish. So on hard bottoms keep the bait bumping bottom and on soft bottoms keep it running free of the bottom and you'll catch more fish.

Naturally, anytime you can ricochet or bounce a crankbait off of something like a brush pile or stump, it will help trigger strikes from bass. Bulldozing these baits into super shallow and shallow brush piles can open up new fishing opportunities for lots of folks.

The Cotton Cordell mid-sized Big O is one of my favorites for this type of fishing along with some of the old square billed balsa baits.

The mid-depth divers account for the majority of baits on the market and fill a large void. These baits can also be very effective thrown in shallow water, 0 to 5 feet range, if you have a fairly hard bottom. They are best however in the 5 to 12 feet range. Naturally the same standards apply for all the crankbait categories as far as stop and go and bumping into objects. In cold water the stop and go is often critical to catching fish.

The deep divers have really gained popularity the last few years and have allowed us to give some of these deep fish a new look. Several manufacturers have models that can be fished in the 12 to 20 foot zone. It is hard to get a bait below 20 feet just by casting. It can be done by trolling but since trolling is not allowed in tournaments, I do not experiment with it. There are a few little things that I feel will help get your baits to run to their maximum depth.

Paul Elias got a lot of people thinking about getting baits deeper when he won the 1982 Bassmaster Classic. They dubbed it "kneeling and reeling." What it amounts to is using a long rod and holding it straight down in the water to force the bait to dive deeper. This definitely helps but something I feel that makes even more difference is the length of the cast and the line diameter. The longer you can cast, the better your opportunity to get the bait deeper. The long rod definitely helps you cast farther. The rod I am currently using for making the long casts and fishing both medium and deep divers is the Team Daiwa 7 foot crankbait rod Rick Clunn designed. It does an excellent job and has a flexible tip action that also allows the bass to inhale the bait a little better. Heavy action rods are a disadvantage in crankbaiting so lighten up for more success.

When I need accuracy with shallow water or the smaller size crankbaits, I use the Team Daiwa rod that George Cochran designed. The new Team Daiwa reels also allow you to make longer casts without the risk of backlashes. I keep my drag adjusted fairly tight while cranking, then I loosen it up once the fish is hooked and close to the boat to help keep the hooks from tearing out. The tight drag helps bury the hooks and the loose drag keeps the fish from pulling out the hook.

Line diameter is very important in getting the bait deeper. The difference between 10 pound and 17 pound line is several feet deeper when cranking with the lighter line. When fishing shallow and medium diving baits I use 8 to 30 pound line for crankbaiting. When fishing the deep divers I almost always use 8 to 12 pound test line. A line I have started

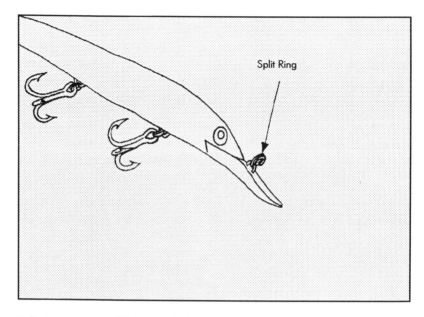

Split Ring

Split rings or snaps will help provide the crankbait with more action. Some crankbaits come from the manufacturer with split rings.

really using for this is 10 pound test Magnathin by DuPont. It has a very thin diameter which helps the bait dig deeper.

Colors of cranks are endless. Early in the year, I throw crawdad colors. In the warmer months and in the fall, I throw shad colored cranks. Naturally at times your chartreuse and red baits can be good depending on water color. The firetiger is one of my best money bait colors and is a great river system color all across the U.S. If someone told me I could take only one crankbait, it would be a Bomber 7A in the firetiger color. Larry Nixon would probably tell you the same as he also has won a ton of money with this bait. The grey ghost color is my favorite shad color.

Although many crankbaits come from the manufacturer with split rings, some do not. With most baits a good split ring or snap will give it more action.

When casting big, heavy plugs retie often as they put a lot of strain on the knots. I also put wide bite hooks on all my crankbaits to help with more hookups. Bomber, Rebel, and several other companies have started putting the wide bite hooks on their lures. A step in the right direction.

Hooks also all need to be sharpened. Every point should be sticky sharp so it grabs ahold and digs into the bass.

Another line of crankbaits that should be mentioned are the vibrating baits. Baits like the Cordells Ratt'l Spot, Bombers Ratl' RRR, etc., are great fish catchers. The 1/2 ounce size is the most popular choice. They are great for winding over the top of vegetation or enticing fish out of weed lines. Chrome with blue back, chrome with black back, and gold with orange belly are my favorite colors. These baits can also be great fished in a drop and jerk fashion to really get them to sound off. They are great baits on schooling fish too.

Crankbaits are super fish locators and no serious bass fisherman should be without a selection of these tools. At times other baits will land more fish once you find them but you have to find them first and few baits are better at that than crankbaits. I know a lot of tournament fishermen simply tie on a crank and start covering water when all else fails.

Topwater

This is as good as it gets. If you don't enjoy catching bass on topwater you might as well start shopping for those golf clubs. Topwater fishing is tremendously exciting although I get pretty revved up when I get a bite on anything. If you have a friend or youngster you want to get interested in bass fishing, wait until a good topwater bite is going and take them fishing.

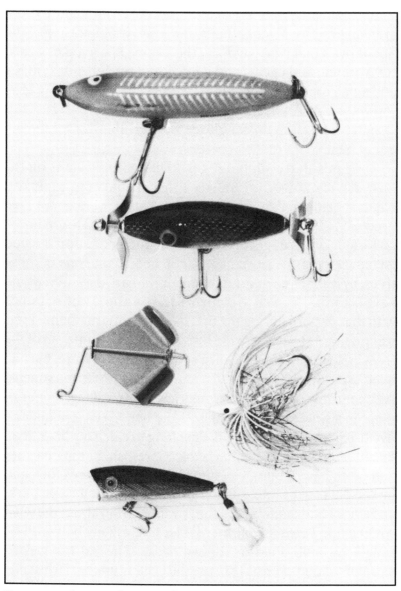

Topwater angling provides some of the most exciting bass fishing. A number of topwater plugs and lures are available to fit various situations.

Equipment wise I like to use the Team Daiwa 7 foot cranking rod for the buzzbaits and large prop baits. For the Spooks and that type bait I like the Team Daiwa rod designed for worming and jigging and it is a 6 foot model. For Pop R's and small topwater, I like the Team Daiwa George Cochran topwater rod. The reel I use is the Team Daiwa TD-1. I use this same reel in all my fishing except when I'm using spinning equipment.

Let's start with buzzbaits. There are all kinds on the market but my favorite is still the original Lunker Lure. It's off balance blade makes a noise the bass just never seem to get tired of. A few years ago while fishing a national tournament on Kentucky Lake I got on a pattern of catching fish on isolated lay-down trees on clay banks. When I could find one of those trees, by itself, say a quarter or half mile apart, each tree would have fish in it. In practice I caught a few on a buzzbait, so I stuck with that pattern during the first day of the tournament. I was using a slow retrieve with the buzzbait and fish came out of the trees in slow motion. It was just a regular Lunker Lure, but had been used enough that it had an unusual high-pitched squeak. All the fish were big, and would just come rolling up out of there in a slow motion and inhale the bait. We were under a five fish limit and it didn't take me long to catch my limit, then I went ahead and caught a couple more fish, but my partner had yet to have a bite. I let him throw into the trees first, and he still didn't get a bite with his buzzbait. I wanted to get back, and since I had made a long run, I was worried about the wind coming up. I told my partner I'd let him use my bait until he caught his limit, then we'd head back. The pattern was so strong we didn't even have to use the trolling motor. I'd just idle up to one of the trees, shut the big motor down and he'd get up front, make a cast across a tree, catch a fish, and I'd head for the next log. Within an hour he had caught his limit, plus a couple more to get rid of a couple of little ones. Then I took my bait back and we headed in. At the weigh-in I was leading the tournament with five fishing weighing 18 pounds.

The next day I went back and caught another limit although not quite as good and dropped to second in the tournament. This, however, shows how important sound can be. He had gone through five or six different buzzbaits of the same size, color, and kind as mine. But that day those fish wanted a bait giving out that particular squeak.

Sound is very important so don't be afraid to mix it up. The regular Lunker Lure is my starting bait but at times you need more noise like the Klak-R-Jak puts out. It has a little lift blade that bangs against the main blade and really makes a racket. You can adjust this noise by bending the lift blade.

The other bait in this group is the Jump'n Jak which is nothing more than a Lunker Lure with a willow leaf blade running behind it. It allows you to buzz the bait up to a stump or other pieces of cover and then let it flutter down like a wounded bait fish. This bait is especially good when a lot of bait fish are in the area.

The main thing to remember is when you think the conditions are right for a buzzbait, start experimenting with the options you have available. Then you better give them what they want and hang on.

With buzzbaits I like the leverage of the 7 foot rod, but a loose tip allowing the fish to get the bait is also a key. You will almost always miss more fish on topwater by jerking too soon than by waiting too long. In fact, it is very important on any topwater explosion to wait a split second before you jerk.

I throw heavy line with buzzbaits, usually 30 pound Stren Magnathin line. This allows me to move fish out of heavy

Buzzbaits are tremendous fish locators. I normally fish buzzbaits on 30 pound test Magnathin line and often add a trailer to provide buoyancy for a slower retrieve.

cover. If I am fishing the bait in open water or just bringing it by cover, I will always use a trailer hook on behind the main hook.

This greatly increases your odds on hookups. If you want to keep the bait up at a slower speed, adding a twin tail trailer or a shaved down pork frog will help give buoyancy and a planing surface.

The colors I prefer are white with silver blade, chartreuse with gold blade, chartreuse with chartreuse blade, and black with black blade. White is best in clear water, chartreuse in stained water, and black in rainy or low light conditions. I like the regular rubber skirts on my buzzbaits and like to keep them fairly short.

Don't be afraid to bump these baits into the sides of

logs, stumps, or the sides of docks to help agitate strikes. Also experiment with speed of retrieve and now and then give the bait an erratic motion.

Buzzbaits are tremendous fish catchers not only for numbers but also for big fish. They are also very easy to use and great to start youngsters with.

These are also great baits for locating bass because you can cover a lot of water. Always, however, keep another rod rigged with a worm, jig, grub, tube bait or something to throw in on a fish if it blows up and misses the buzzbait. A quick cast right to the spot with a back-up lure can be very effective.

I have been on some great topwater bites over the years but the problem is having the weather hold up stable enough for a multiple day tournament. Normally there are weather changes during tournaments and topwater patterns are usually the first to appear or disappear. That is one reason you don't see a lot of tournaments won strictly on topwater baits. They are, however, very important and can not be beat when they are right. I have really developed a lot of confidence in certain topwater baits and they will always have a place in my big old Plano tackle box.

The Lunker Lure (especially the 3/8 and 1/2 ounce sizes) is a true favorite but I also have others that help me fish all the topwater situations.

The Zara Spook is probably the most famous topwater bait of all. This bait, made by Heddon, has been around for years and is a valuable tool when used properly. It is also one of the best big bass baits. I like to fish it in calm water but have had success in water with a slight chop. The key is figuring out how the bass want it. At times they want it worked real fast like a bait fish and other times it takes a slosh, slosh, and stop technique. The rod action is back and forth and is very easy to master especially with the right rod. I like to use Larry Nixon's Team Daiwa rod in the 6 foot model. It is stiff enough to make the bait do what I want it to do yet light enough that I don't get tired maneuvering the lure.

As far as line, I love to use 14 pound test regular, clear Stren. In ultra clear water I might go as low as 10 pound test and in stained water as high as 17 pound test. I normally tie a loop knot so the Spook works a little easier. The regular original size is about the only one I use although lots of success has been had on the little Zara Puppy. I also prefer the common, over-the-counter, new plastic version over the old wood baits. The hooks hitting against the plastic make more noise and help attract strikes.

Some people take split rings and attach the hooks to the bait. They claim this helps them land more fish. If you are having trouble losing fish on a Spook, you might give this a try. Some of the most vicious strikes I have ever had have come on a Spook, so brace yourself when you throw one.

You need a lot of self discipline and concentration to keep from occasionally taking the bait away from fish. At times they will blow up on it four or five times before they finally take it. So just keep working it until you feel resistance and then load the rod up with pressure.

I love to fish this bait and carry a lot of different colors. Because it stays in the strike zone longer, colors really seem to make a difference. Some favorites are the bullfrog and perch in stained water and the Christmas tree and blue shore minnow in clear water. I have also done well with the chrome and the clear Spook in clear water. The black Spook has been good in low light conditions and at night. The bright perch color has been great for me around areas for smallmouth.

The Spook is also good in clear water because you can

throw it so far. It can be just as dangerous if you miss a fish as it flies back just as well. You should always wear a good pair of sunglasses or protective glasses when fishing to protect your eyes from flying lures, especially when topwater fishing.

There are other walking type baits on the market but as of now, the Spook is still my favorite and the only one I use.

Another good money bait for me has been the Pop R by Rebel. This bait, when worked correctly, is a great numbers bait. It will catch lots of fish and has a high hookup rate. It is small enough most bass get it in their mouths well and you don't lose many fish. You can catch fish on it working it slow but it is really at its best worked fast in an erratic type motion. I use a lot of the same action as when I work the Spook, but faster.

Again, I like the George Cochran Team Daiwa topwater rod with its softer tip for this. In line size 12 to 14 pound test clear Stren are my favorites although I have used heavier line when working the Pop R fast over heavy bushes and vegetation. This bait seems to be at its best in clear water. I especially like it around milfoil and hydrilla beds. You try to make it act like a fleeing bait fish (spitting water forward as you work it) escaping from another game fish. This brings out the competitive nature of the bass. The spitting sound is very important. If you have ever watched shad working and being chased, this is the sound you are after. It takes a little while to develop the correct sound and technique.

Zell Rowland, who helped popularize this bait by winning a major BASS Tournament on it, showed me a lot about the bait. I know of no one that is any better at working this bait than Zell. He totally understands what the bait is supposed to do and is deadly when bass are on a Pop R bite. If you are having trouble getting the bait to act right, you might shave a little off the bottom lip and also keep your knot at the lower

The Pop R by Rebel is one of the best topwater baits because it has a high hook-up rate. It can sometimes be made more productive by shaving off the bottom lip and tieing your line knot on the lower side of the wire tie loop.

side of the wire tie loop. This helps give it lift.

As far as colors, the chrome/black back and chrome/blue back are the standbys. However, I have had excellent luck on a bluegill pattern that Zell painted for me and also the new G-finish that Pradco Lures has come out with. In clear water, the G-finish in the grays, aqua, and blues are excellent. I have caught bass up to 9 pounds on the Pop R but it is more noted for being a numbers bait. Just remember the key normally is working this bait in a fast, erratic motion.

One other bait that has been good to me is the Wood-chopper. This is a prop bait with stainless steel blades that really disturb the water. It can be great worked in a jerk, jerk, stop fashion. Just remember that your line does take abuse

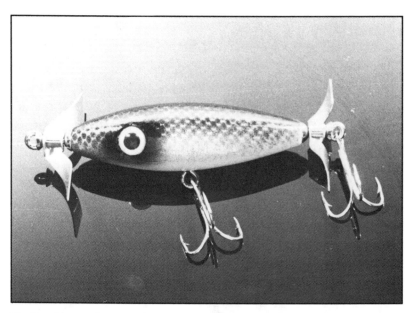

The Woodchopper from Ozark Mountain Tackle Co. is an extremely effective prop bait. It is a heavy bait, can be thrown great distances, and used in rough water.

from this bait. This is a heavy bait (I like the large size) so you can throw it a long ways. This bait is my favorite for working in rough water and big waves. In warm water try getting on a bank with the waves crashing in on it and throw this big prop bait. Hang onto your cap because the action can be fast and furious.

Topwater baits are fascinating and fun to fish and we could discuss lots of them but these are my favorites and the ones I primarily use. I am sure many of the other baits will accomplish the same results. Just find some to fill the different situations, develop confidence in them, and you're on your way to some exciting bass fishing.

> **Tip--Using the right rod and proper timing on your hook set are also extremely important in topwater fishing.**

Spinnerbaits

Spinnerbaits come in endless shapes, sizes, and colors. Everyone has their favorites and lots of fishermen make their spinnerbaits at home. Spinnerbaits are extremely versatile and because of this we're probably guilty of not fishing them as much as we should. This bait can be fished in any weather situation and any time of year, depending on the model.

If I am making long casts, I use the same 7 foot Team Daiwa Crankin' rod that I throw Lunker Lures with. If I'm fishing the bait close and in heavy cover where casting accuracy is critical, I use the Team Daiwa 6 or 6 1/2 foot Worming/Jigging rod. Line sizes vary from 10 to 30 pounds depending on the cover and water clarity. I usually use 30 pound Magnathin

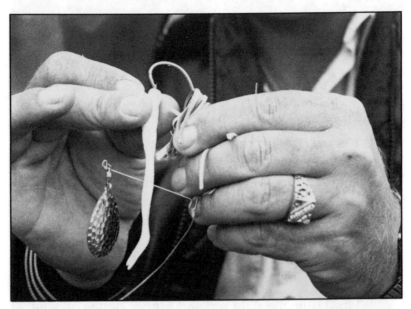

Spinnerbaits are one of the most versatile lures. They can be used slow, fast, deep or shallow or anywhere between and are available in countless sizes and colors.

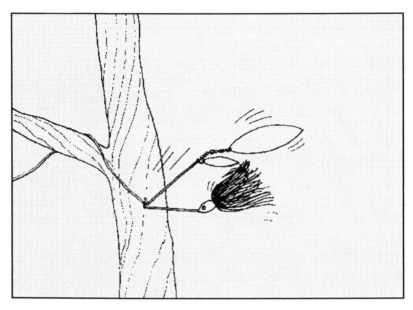

A variety of techniques can be used with spinnerbaits. One of my favorites is to reel it up to an object, then let it drop a couple of counts before moving it again.

with spinnerbaits. Always try to bump objects with the bait and make it do something erratic to entice a strike.

One technique is reeling a spinnerbait up to an object then letting it drop a couple of counts before moving it again. This dropping action often gets the bass to commit to the bait. I have also done well with single spins by letting them free fall to the bottom and then reeling them in slow but still keeping contact with the bottom and having the blade turn. This is great in colder water.

A black skirted spinnerbait with a nickel blade is my favorite for this bottom dragging. A 3/8 ounce with a #5 Colorado blade is my favorite but if you go very deep you may want to go to a heavier weight head.

I prefer to use white, chartreuse, or white/chartreuse

combinations on all spinnerbaits I fish off the bottom. At times a little blue or gold mixed in the skirts can be good. In clear water use white with nickel blades. In stained water use chartreuse with chartreuse blades, and the same around clear water smallmouth areas.

For crawling and working around brush piles and heavy wood cover, the single spin is best but around vegetation I prefer willow leaf blade patterns. A #5 or #6 willow leaf blade with a small Colorado blade in front is a great grass bait, giving off lots of flash. Also two willow leaf blades in tandem are good but don't throw as well. These baits work best for me on a steady retrieve. Alternate the retrieve speed until you find what gets the best results. If the lake or river I'm fishing is tough and bites are hard to get, especially by good fish, I'll down size my spinnerbait and throw 1/4 ounce baits, often with just a simple #4 willow leaf blade.

At times bass want a subtle, quiet spinner and other times a loud, vibrating bait. The rule I use--subtle, quiet baits in clear water and loud vibration in stained and dirty water.

Vibration is very important so play around with different blades. Get some good spinnerbaits that are balanced well and learn to fish them in all conditions. I use trailer hooks when getting snagged is not a major factor. I also usually have some sort of plastic trailer. Bass Pro makes a great Twin Tail Trailer and so does Burke.

Strike King Lures produces a unique spinnerbait blade called the Tennessee Diamond. Embossed with a highly-reflective diamond pattern, this unusual blade produces 20% more vibration and 4-1/2 times more flash than conventional blades.

A localized bait, the Pomme Special from MarLynn, can also be dynamite for bringing fish up out of cover. It is a single spin designed for gurgling the water with a great sound.

Don't forget the Beetle Spin types and also the small in-lines like the Mepps. These are great with light line in fairly open water and good baits for limits, especially around smallmouths. I also always carry a few Hildebrandt Snagless Sally's for fishing in heavy vegetation. They come through it very well.

Overall, spinnerbaits are a great line of fish catchers, great fish locators, and good baits for probing heavy cover.

Tip---Spend time winding spinnerbaits at a speed so that you can just see them coming in the water. I like to keep a spinnerbait barely in sight all the way in. I often see fish actually hit the bait.

Worms, Lizards, and Crawdads

If you took the plastic worms out of the average tournament anglers boat it would probably run 5 mph faster. This may be an exaggeration but most anglers carry a bunch. They come in so many sizes and colors it gets hard to cut back. I try to take only those necessary for the area I am fishing. If I'm going to Florida, I have big worms and some straight tail worms for penetrating the heavy cover. I also have colors like black grape, black and blue, red shad, and junebug. If I'm going to Lake Mead out in the desert, I'll pack worms in the 3 to 6 inch range. The little 4 inch doodle worms and ringworms are excellent. The silvers, smokes, and grape with red flake are good choices. Certain areas dictate the use of certain sizes and colors. Do your research but be willing to experiment.

I feel the straight and ribbon tail worms are best in clear water. The hook tail type worms put out greater pressure waves and are better in stained and dirty water.

Naturally the most popular way of fishing worms is the traditional Texas rig. There are, however, lots of other ways that you should learn to fish worms to match certain situations. Most of the time when I'm Texas rigged I use slip sinkers from 1/8 to 3/8 ounce, depending on the fishing depth. An example would be a 1/8 ounce slip sinker, a 1/0 hook, and a 4 to 6-inch worm. Match the hook to the worm. On a 7 to 10-inch worm I use a 4/0 to 5/0 hook. Line size runs from 6 to 30 pounds depending on the cover and technique being used.

I fish small worms on a 6 1/2 foot Team Daiwa rod with the Team Daiwa spinning reel. The larger worms I cast on Larry Nixon's Team Daiwa 6 1/2 foot worming rod. I love to use this rod with 14 pound test Stren line. I use the clear line but if you have trouble seeing your line, you might try the clear blue

Plastic worms, lizards, and crawdads are available in a multitude of sizes, shapes, and colors and can be rigged in a variety of ways to catch bass almost anywhere or time.

fluorescent Stren to help you watch your line and detect strikes better.

Learn to know what your worm is doing at all times. Anytime you're not sure what your bait is doing, set the hook. Experiment with retrieves. At times the bass wants it dragged on the bottom, other times they want it pumped up off the bottom and moving more. Try different presentations. When I guided I'd have clients throw the worm out and swim it back in and still catch fish. Normally the colder the water the slower the presentation. As the water warms, you can put more action in your retrieves.

When I fish visible cover, I prefer a regular Texas rig. The last couple of years, however, I have started using Carolina rigged worms quite a bit and have had good success with

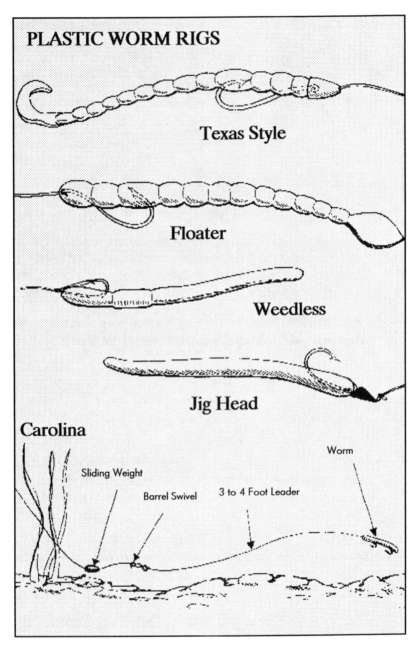

PLASTIC WORM RIGS

Texas Style

Floater

Weedless

Jig Head

Carolina

Sliding Weight

Barrel Swivel

3 to 4 Foot Leader

Worm

both worms and lizards. A 6-inch Zoom or Bass Pro lizard fished on a Carolina rig can be hard to beat when fishing points and structure spots.

I think the Carolina rig allows the lizard to look more natural. Once in a while I fish a lizard Texas rigged in shallow water (especially during spawning season) but I always fish light slip sinkers with it. Some of my favorite lizard colors are black with chartreuse tail, black with blue tail, pumpkinseed, green gourd, and cotton candy.

Plastic crawdads have become popular in the last few years and can be great Texas or Carolina rigged. They come in a variety of colors to match your selection to the conditions.

Floating worms and lizards have also started to get exposure. I have been fishing the bright colored floating worms for several years and really hate to see this technique get popular. It is a great way to catch fish in shallow water when they are not biting well. I like a 6-inch worm with a 4/0 hook on 10 to 17 pound test line depending on water clarity. Just twitch it along and let it stop and start to sink occasionally. When the fish hits, let them have it a second and then set the hook hard.

I set the hook hard with all worm fishing. I set the hook with some slack in the line so that I can pop the hook into the fish a little better. With a little practice you can get your timing right. I always set the hook once, keep the line tight, and never allow the fish any slack line to throw the bait. I never toothpick a slipsinker when casting worms. I use straight shank worm hooks with the little barbs to help hold the worm in place.

Worm hooks, just like any hook, need to be super sharp. I run the hook back and forth through the worm to make a little tunnel so that it slides into the fish easier on the hook set. Also a little tournament trick is to put several glass rattles inside the worm, lizard or crawdad. This really helps in heavy

One tournament trick I've discovered is to insert several tiny glass rattles into the worm, lizard or crawdad. It really helps in heavy cover.

cover and will give you an edge over your competitors.

We could do a whole book just on worm fishing, but hopefully we have hit on a thing or two here that will help put more fish on your worms. Worms are great baits so get out and develop confidence in using them. Larry Nixon is proof of the type of success that can be attained with efficient worm fishing. Larry is an excellent and versatile angler with all types of lures and techniques, but when a good worm bite is going on just plan on him taking another wheelbarrow of money to the bank.

Finesse Lures

We could get carried away in this section so I'll try to keep it short and just go into the baits and techniques I primarily use the majority of the time.

Light line fishing and finesse lures has grown in popularity the last few years and will continue to do so as lakes get increased fishing pressure. Finesse lures are great around high pressure fishing areas and also in clear water situations.

The tube lure types have been dynamite for several years and continue to be good. Tube lures can be rigged different ways with several different head styles. In shallow water I prefer lightweight heads that allow the bait to spiral to the bottom. I fish these baits and almost all finesse baits on the 6 or 6 1/2 foot Team Daiwa spinning rod. I use 6 to 10 pound test clear Stren or Magnathin line.

Tube baits are great to throw on visible fish and great as back up lures to topwater explosions. You can put a little piece of cork inside a tube bait and make it a neat little topwater bait for skipping around boat docks and grass beds. In clear water I like the silver sparkle and smoke colors that do a good job of imitating minnows and bait fish. I have had excellent luck in stained water with the pumpkinseed color. Chartreuse with silver flake has been great for smallmouth. The skipping technique with the tube baits is great in shallow water as it seems to draw bass and excite them. Keep in mind that with the tube baits the majority of your strikes will come on the fall.

My next favorite light-line bait is the grub, a bait that has really been improved the last few years. Kalin Lures has a great 5-inch grub on the market and Bass Pro also has several that do good jobs. Oldham Lures have some excellent jig heads, both regular and with wire weed guards, to use with these grubs.

I occasionally throw this bait on baitcasting equipment using Cochran's rod and 10 pound test Magnathin. Grubs in 3

Finesse fishing with light line and tiny finesse lures has quickly become one of the most productive fishing tactics, especially on highly pressured lakes and reservoirs.

and 5-inch sizes are great largemouth and smallmouth lures. Great numbers baits. No tournament angler should go out without a rod rigged with a tube bait or grub. My favorite grub colors are salt and pepper with silver flake, pumpkinseed, and smoke. I Carolina rig the grubs now and then, usually in river situations, on points, and bass that are in current.

The 3 and 4-inch worms also fall in this group. Don Ivino popularized the doodle technique and Gary Klein added to it with a couple of BASS victories using this method. It involves shaking one of these little baits on light line in deep water. Normally a 3/16 ounce slip sinker is used and at times a glass bead is placed between it and the hook to add sound and protect the knot. This is also great on Kentucky bass, especially when they're in deep brush piles or around deep boat docks.

116

FINESSE LURES

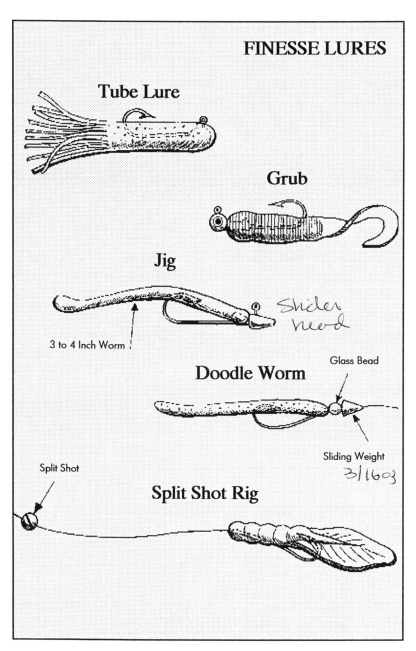

Tube Lure

Grub

Jig

Slider head

3 to 4 Inch Worm

Doodle Worm

Glass Bead

Sliding Weight

3/16oz

Split Shot

Split Shot Rig

Split-shoting is a fairly new method that I have used lately and really like. Some of the small reaper type baits are great with this method.

When using these light lines and baits, lots of times you will just feel something heavy. Don't jerk too hard, just pull back and keep the pressure even. The fine wire hooks should penetrate without a problem. Sometimes fish hooked in deep water will come off when they jump. One remedy is to file the barb off the hook so that it penetrates easier and deeper. Then just make sure the fish doesn't get any slack.

Light line requires a properly set drag, good knots, sharp hooks, and keeping your cool during the fight. I like to back-reel or loosen my drag when fighting a fish close to the boat. This makes it hard for them to break off. In some tournaments we can't use nets so we get in the habit of swinging well-hooked fish into the boat. Keep in mind with light line you best lip or belly land these bass for safety sake. A lot of fish are lost at the boat by people that lose their head at the last second.

In order to be a completely versatile fisherman you should master light line and finesse fishing. It will provide you with another tactic for more consistent bass catching.

The Jig and Frog

When I started fishing the jig-and-frog I realized in a hurry that it was the best big bass bait I had ever thrown. The jig and frog is also one of the hardest baits for people to get adept at using and develop confidence in. There has, however, been more tournament money won on a jig than any other bait in the last 10 years. Part of the reason is because the jig is so versatile. It can be fished at any depth and under almost any conditions using a wide variety of techniques.

A jig-and-frog is the best big bass bait available. My favorites, of course, are the Bootlegger Jigs from Strike King Lures.

Bass will still bite a jig even in adverse cold front conditions when other baits drop off. The jig-and-frog has accounted for a bunch of my tournament wins, and my fun meter definitely pegs when a good jig bite is on in a tournament. The success I have had with this bait has helped me develop several theories on jig fishing.

Several things are necessary for an effective jig. The bend of the hook is important so the top edge of the hook remains parallel with the shank of the hook for good hook sets. The line-tie eye must be turned sideways and this does two things. First it helps the bait ride over and through cover without turning sideways and getting hung up. And second it gives you a bigger hooking throat which allows more hookups.

The hook on these jigs, such as the Strike King Bootlegger Jigs, is designed for flipping but I have used it for casting with line as light as 10 pound test and had no problems hooking. Some jigs are available in a thinner diameter hook for casting and easier penetration with light line. They can easily be fished on line from 16 to 20 pound test. I do, however, recommend using the heavier hooks on 14 to 40 pound test.

These jigs are normally available in 1/8, 1/4, 3/8, 1/2, 5/8 and sometimes 3/4 and a full one-ounce. The 3/8 ounce is my favorite but they all have their place. Live rubber skirts are popular, but the silicone skirts, such as the Bootlegger with Strike King's exclusive "Mirage" silicone skirt has the uncanny ability of changing colors in varying light and water clarities. The Bootlegger Jig is available in numerous "Mirage" colors and all sizes feature the Eagle Claw Lazer-Sharp hooks, sparkling Diamond Dust head finishes and nylon bristle weedguards. My favorite color is Black Perch. This is good in all water color situations but especially good in fairly clear water. In dirty water I like black with a few strands of chartreuse or yellow which is the Strike King Texas Craw color. All black is good under any water color condition. Brown with copper is great on tidal waters and has been a good color for me in the eastern states. Black with bright green has been good in a lot of areas including Florida. Black with red has been good on the east Texas lakes along with the black with chartreuse. You really do need a good selection of weights and colors to match different areas and situations.

The standard Bootlegger Jig, long recognized by many pro anglers as the jig of choice has been greatly improved with a unique rattler which adds the dimension of sound to help attract fish. The rattle also holds the plastic crawdad type trailers securely in place and helps keep the pork frog back on the bend of the hook where it belongs. Real aggressive fish will often push the pork in front of the hook and you hook the frog rather than the fish. This doesn't happen often, but in a tournament situation, once is too often and the rattle eliminates this.

You can take a small piece of worm and thread it on before you add your frog and this will also do the trick.

Jigs must have a strong fiber weedguard to keep them from hanging up. When one does wedge, remember the bow and arrow technique to free it.

When I fish a heavier hooked flipping jig on lighter line, I cut some of the fiber strands out of the weedguard and bend the barb down so it penetrates easier. The weedguard on some jigs comes pre-trimmed for length which makes it more compact and gives you better hookups on fish. Irregardless of what jig you use, if it doesn't work in heavy cover you better look for another brand.

As far as trailers to go behind the jig, there are many kinds that can be used for different situations. In water temperatures from 40 to 70 degrees I almost always use Strike King's Pig Tail Trailer. Whether it is just confidence in the produce or what, fish just seem to bite it and hang on better.

I fish the pork right out of the jar doing nothing fancy to it. Regardless if I'm flipping or casting or even using a small jig on light line with spinning equipment, I prefer the Pig Tail Trailer because it is precision die cut with swimming legs which produce far more life-like action than similar baits and it is extremely soft yet durable. Some fishermen trim their pork and if it works for you, do it. I personally like them right from the jar and believe me, so do the bass.

There are a couple of little tricks you can use to increase productivity of the pig-and-jig. A couple of days before your tournament or fishing trip, pour out part of the solution the frogs are kept in and fill the jar up with your favorite fish scent. I also like to add a little salt. Keep in mind, however, that the solution the frogs were stored in was there to preserve them and when you alter it you shorten the time period before they spoil.

I also change frogs several times during the day. Not only does this give me a bait with more scent, but it also gives me a brighter bait. Most frogs fade after being fished for a period of time and lose some of their effectiveness.

I always hook the frog by pushing the hook through the fatty side first. This keeps the fatty belly of the frog down when you are fishing, giving it a more natural action and appearance. It also helps open up the hooking throat of the jig even more. Some frogs are two-toned with the fatty side the lighter colored side. Everything that swims in the water whether it is a bait fish, bluegill or crawdad has a lighter underside. By hooking the frog through the fat first you guarantee this natural look.

I use lots of other forms of Strike King pork as well. Around spawning season or when I want a bait that will penetrate vegetation a little easier, I use the Bo-Hawg Frog as a trailer.

In late summer and fall when the bass are actively feeding on shad in certain reservoirs, take a white or gray jig and a Bo-Hawg Frog of the same color and fish it for suspended fish in timber--it can be awesome.

At times I use plastic trailers. Some of the plastic crawdads make pretty good jig trailers, allowing you to mix up the colors more and even giving a metal flake look.

I helped Bass Pro design one with rattle chambers in the claws to provide even more noise. Others that I have used with good success are the Craw-Worm, Big Claw, Salt Craw, and the Guido Bug. I do better with the plastic trailers during the warmer months than the other times of the year.

About the only other trailer I use behind a jig is a worm. This can be great when fishing it deep and also great on suspended fish. A worm with a ripple type action like Bass Pro's Tripple Ripple in the 5-inch size is an excellent deep jig trailer. At times I will even bite an inch off the worm to help it drop faster. In shallow or stained water, I like a G-tail type worm like the old 5-inch Gator Tail for a trailer.

My favorite pork colors are black, black and blue, black and chartreuse, brown, and white. My favorite plastic crawdad colors are black and blue, black and chartreuse, pumpkinseed, and fire and ice. My favorite worm trailer colors are black and blue, black and chartreuse, pumpkinseed, junebug, and red.

These are the different bait combinations and as I said earlier, they can be fished in a lot of different ways. A jig and trailer is a very versatile lure. It can be buzzed across the top through bushes in clear water and attract some vicious strikes. This is a great spring technique on certain lakes, especially the desert lakes. When buzzing a jig through the tops of trees and bushes, keep your rod tip high and when the fish hits, drop your rod tip down allowing the fish to get the bait and turn--then jerk his head off.

The most common way to fish a jig is just casting it. Flipping and pitching jigs is also very popular but we'll discuss that in the flipping section. Cast fishing a jig is not much different than fishing a worm. I like Larry Nixon's Team Daiwa Worming rod best for this. On occasions if I'm fishing a jig real deep or making long casts, I'll use my flipping rod for casting so I can take up even more line on the hookset. Remember the hookset needs to be hard to guarantee good hook penetration. I fish line from 8 to 40 pound test with jigs but the majority of the time I cast a jig on 10 to 17 pound line depending on water clarity and cover density.

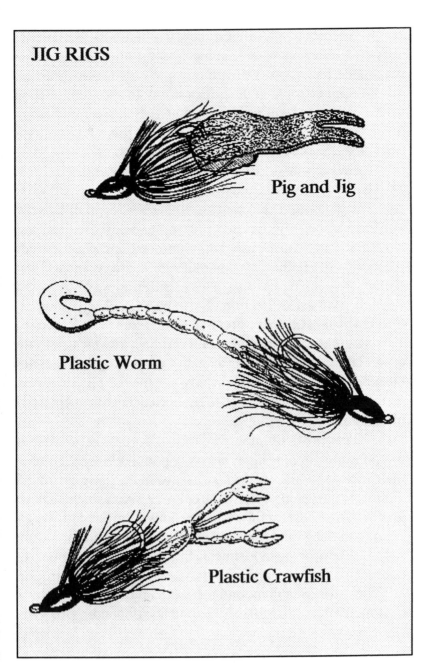

JIG RIGS

Pig and Jig

Plastic Worm

Plastic Crawfish

I always try to let a jig fall on a controlled drop. In other words it is falling on a slack line but you are still aware of what it is doing. This is important because a good percentage of your strikes come on the fall. Watch your line closely and if it does anything strange, set the hook. I don't believe in getting into feeling contact with bass (letting the bass run with the bait) when jig fishing. They can spit it out pretty fast when they want to, so put the steel to them fast if you even suspect a strike. It doesn't cost anything to jerk but it could if you don't. You'll feel when the jig hits bottom. Concentrate on your bait and what it's doing. That's what makes a good jig fisherman.

After it hits bottom, I pause a second then lift the rod and sense for any weight. If it feels heavy, I drop the rod and set the hook. If it feels normal, I move the jig. The colder the water, the slower I work the jig. In warm water I often sweep it off the bottom quite a ways and swim it more. Every time I move the bait, I repeat this system of sensing for weight. Because of a jigs buoyancy (especially when fished with a pork frog), fish can inhale it very subtly. That is why it is so important to be on the lookout for any heavy feel to the bait.

Naturally the deeper you fish, the harder it is to sense this. I go to heavier jigs as I progress deeper to give me a greater awareness of what my bait is doing. If you do detect a strike and miss the fish, don't reel in, just let the bait drop back down and resume working it normally. Lots of times (especially smallmouth) bass will come right back and strike again. The more you fish a jig the more confidence you gain in it. At times there will be other baits that might get more strikes but very few will give you the quality catch that the jig will.

If you have never caught a bass over 5 pounds, I would suggest you start fishing a jig-and-frog. I'd almost bet you'll see the size of the bass you are catching increase. The first day I fished a jig-and-frog, I caught two 6 pounders on back-to-back casts. Since that time I think I've won more money with that bait than any other angler. If you ever have any thoughts of fishing for a living, it is a must to master the jig in order to be consistently competitive.

Spoons (Jigging and Grass)

First let's talk a little about jigging spoons. When the weather is at its extremes, the spoon is best. Real cold water and real warm water normally find me digging out a spoon. The old CC Spoon is a favorite in the 1/2 and 1 ounce models. Chrome is my favorite spoon color although I have done well with gold on cloudy days.

I always fish a jigging spoon straight under the boat at whatever level I find fish. The colder the water, the slower I work it. At times just holding it still, letting it unwind on the line, and allowing the movement of the boat to impart the action. At other times if I'm fishing it on the bottom, I let it just flop back and forth. In warm water I pop it pretty good and at times sweep the rod three feet moving the bait up and down. I like to put oversize hooks on my spoons and also a good split ring for the line tie to help cut down on knot fatigue. I have seen the spoon produce well all across the country. On Thousand Islands in New York for smallmouth along deep grass lines, and also along current points in the river itself in 60 feet of water--at times you would catch a fish every drop. On Toledo Bend dropping the spoon down in the hardwoods along the main river channel has been extremely good.

With just a little practice, it is amazing how you can fish a spoon without getting it hung. Rather than pulling when the bait wedges or the hooks stick, jiggle your rod and the spoon

126

Jigging spoons are at their best when the weather is extremely cold or extremely hot. One trick I have discovered is shoving a jigging spoon up inside a tube lure.

itself normally acts as a plug knocker. Once again, especially when jigging trees, it is critical to pay attention and figure out what depth the fish are holding.

I normally let a spoon go straight to the bottom and jig it for a little while. If I don't get any action, I take about three turns on the reel handle and jig a little at that depth. I keep repeating this until I contact fish and then I know how to get my bait exactly to the strike zone. I have seen the spoon produce excellent results in tournaments on both Sidney Lanier and West Point Lake in Georgia. The spoon is also good for big Kentucky spotted bass on Table Rock Lake in Missouri where, in the late fall and winter, you can take a spoon on the bluff points and go wild. You can also get on the long gravel flat points that run out toward the river channel and look for bait.

Several tactics can be used with the jigging spoon, but I normally let it go straight to the bottom, jig it a little bit, then continue raising and jigging until I contact fish.

When you spot swarms of bait fish on your electronics, drop a spoon to their level and start jigging. There are almost always good Kentuckies relating to these shad that can be caught with a spoon. About any lake in the country with bridge pillars is also a likely candidate for spoons.

Another little trick I use in clear water and also for schooling fish is to take a spoon and shove it up inside a tube lure. It really looks good and you can do endless things with color plus give the bass a more natural feeling bait to hit. You can also throw this combination a long ways to schools of surfacing fish and jerk it back with good results. Plus you can fill the tube with scent.

A jigging spoon may not be very attractive or fun to use but it is an excellent fishing tool deserving a spot in your tackle box.

Grass Spoons

The surface and grass spoons on the other hand are popular and can be extremely exciting to use. Bassmaster TV did a couple of shows featuring Rat fishing which showed fishermen how exciting fishing frogs, rats, and spoon type grass baits could be.

Naturally, timing on your hookset is just like fishing topwater baits. Don't jerk too soon. I use the Team Daiwa 7 foot cranking rod to fish these grass baits and spoons. I use 30 pound test Magnathin line to make sure I get the fish out after the hit. The biggest stringer I ever weighed in during a BASS tournament came on a 1/2 ounce Johnson Spoon (chrome) with a white Bass Pro twin tail trailer. If high winds had not ruined the area and kept me from fishing it the last day, I think I would have won. But that's tournament fishing and another reason to have backup patterns when possible. This was on Okeechobee Lake in Florida, one of the best big bass spoon lakes anywhere. I was keeping the spoon 6 inches below the surface working it through pepper-grass flats. I used the wind to push my boat across the grass flats, fan casting as it drifted. I saw every fish come out and hit the spoon--talk about fun.

Another spoon that comes through the cover great is the Rebel Arrowhead spoon. It has a little tighter wobble and is a better producer during adverse weather. The Snakie Spoon is another good grass spoon and comes in a variety of good colors. A bait that earned a permanent spot in my Plano box is the Rebel Moss Boss. I fished this spoon on the Hudson River in New York and caught over 30 bass between 3 and 5 pounds without moving the boat. I hit the tide just right in a grassbed and had a field day. I twitched the spoon in little quick jerks (almost like working a Spook) that made it jump up

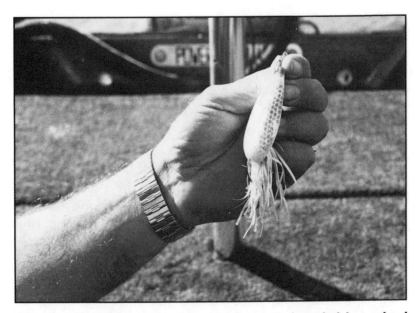

Dancing a Rebel Moss Boss in short hops across the moss and grass beds has produced a lot of big bass for me.

and down and caused a squeak between the metal snap and plastic spoon. Since then this technique of short hopping (or dancing) a Moss Boss has put a lot of good bass in the boat for me. I like the green spotted Moss Boss the best.

One little trick for higher hooking percentages with the Arrowhead and Johnson type spoons is using pliers to open up the hook a little. It is still very weedless this way but catches more bass.

Jerkbaits, Twitchbaits, and Stickbaits

Jerkbaits, twitchbaits, and stickbaits are all proven bass catchers. I like a 5 1/2 to 6 foot medium heavy rod for fishing these baits. The rod must be comfortable because worked

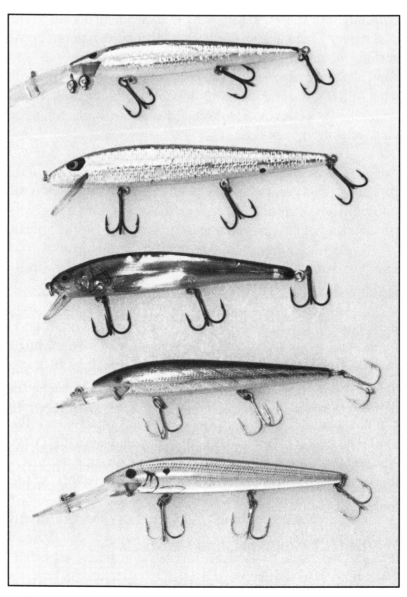

Jerkbaits, stickbaits, and twitchbaits are all fantastic bass catchers. They are especially effective used extremely slow in the cold water of winter.

correctly your wrist and arm will be ready to fall off at the end of the day. The majority of the time I keep the bait under the surface moving it along in short, sharp jerks. At times the fish want it in big hard jerks and when this happens I usually go with a big #18 Rapala and jerk it hard with my flipping stick. Silver with black back on cloudy days and silver with blue back on clear days are my choices.

The bait I jerk the most during the year is the Bomber Long A. This is a very stable, durable bait and a favorite of pros. It is also a great smallmouth lure. My favorite color is the one with the gold insert. Of course, the silver insert is also very good and any of the chartreuse patterns are good for smallmouth.

The A.C. Shiner in the smaller sizes is also a good numbers bait. The Rogue in certain models is also pretty popular.

This section certainly would not be complete without talking about the Spoonbill Rebel. Rebel makes other good minnow baits but the Spoonbill is my favorite. This bait can be pulled through the water when it is cold similar to fishing a worm, or jerked in the conventional manner. It is a great big-fish bait. In early spring when fish are first moving up, this bait can be dynamite. There really are no bad times to work this bait. The best conditions are cloudy or windy days but I have also had some good days just twitching one of these baits near the surface when fish are up very shallow. I like working this bait on clear line in the 10 to 14 pound range.

I have seen guys go to all kinds of extremes to properly weight jerkbaits so that they have natural buoyancy. This can make some of the baits more successful at times, especially when the water is still cold and you need to keep the bait in a certain zone longer to entice strikes. I had a Missouri angler, by the name of Larry Baker, work some stickbaits up for me a couple of times and had excellent success with them. He put new bills on them, weighted them, and repainted them.

For the majority of the fishermen, however, baits straight from the factory are very effective. The biggest reason I have a fond spot for Larry's tuned stickbaits is that the first time I really fished one was when I drew out with him in a major tournament. He gave me one to use and I was leading at the end of the day. I had three bass that weighed 17 pounds including an 8 pounder. If I had been better at playing fish way back then, I'd have weighed a 5-fish limit in the 25 to 27 pound range and put the tournament away.

That is how you get better, by getting that on-the-water experience. We learn from both good and bad days on the water and move on, better educated and hopefully, more consistent. Jerkbaits have accounted for some great stringers of bass weighed in over the years by anglers like Basil Bacon, Jimmy Crisp, Gary Klein, and others. In recent years Jim Bitter of Florida has shown that the jerkbaits can catch fish all across the country.

When fish want the bait jerked hard it is probably one of the most difficult techniques in fishing as far as being fatiguing and hard on the body, but it can also be one of the most productive.

I hope this section on lures and how I and others use them has been helpful. Just keep in mind that lures are all tools designed to do different jobs. The more tools you can handle efficiently and develop confidence in, the more consistent and successful your fishing will be.

Tip--Wide-bite, razor sharp hooks will greatly increase your catch with stickbaits.

Flippin' and pitchin' are extremely effective methods for catching bass in many situations and have provided me with a lot of big bass, and tournament wins.

Chapter 5

FLIPPING AND PITCHING

The Proper Equipment

The first requirement is to find a rod that is right for you. If you are short, a 7 foot rod may be the ticket. If you are tall, you may want an 8 foot rod. I am 6' 2" and use a 7 1/2 foot rod. I really think it is what you get used to and that for overall efficiency the 7 1/2 foot rod is the best.

I didn't know much about rods until Daiwa gave me the opportunity to design their flipping and pitching rods. It was quite an experience working with engineers, getting just the right action and weights, lengths, diameters, etc. I designed two rods; one for flipping/pitching and one for heavy flipping.

I must admit, the flipping/pitching rod is the one I use almost 100% of the time. I learned a long time ago that cover is not often uniform. Seldom are you just flipping or just pitching. It never made sense to me to continually be switching rods as the cover changed. That is why I designed a rod that was right for both. It has a tip that is light enough to give you distance and the control needed to pitch. The soft tip action also helps cushion your hookset when flipping and keeps you from breaking your line. Yet the rod has all the backbone you need for flipping and moving fish out of heavy cover.

Having a rod you can both pitch and flip with is especially important when fishing tournaments, where time is critical. You are just so much more efficient when one rod can do both.

The rod I fish most of the time is called "Denny Brauer's Flippin'/Pitchin' Team Daiwa Rod." My second rod is called "Denny Brauer's Flippin' Team Daiwa Rod" but I use it only when I'm flipping heavy mats of vegetation.

I feel that the majority of the fish lost while flipping and pitching is because people are using improper equipment. In most cases I think they're using too stiff a rod and breaking line or tearing too big a hole in the fishes mouth so that as soon as it sticks its head out of the water, the bait comes out. I consistently set the hook really hard every time and let the soft tip of my flippin'/pitchin' rod act as a shock absorber.

I use the TD-1 Team Daiwa reel for flipping/pitching. This is the same reel that I use with everything but spinning. It has a flipping feature or switch but I don't use it because I'm left-handed and don't have to switch hands during a presentation. If you fish right handed, this switch may be handy for you. Just remember, however, the simpler you can keep your fishing, the less room for error.

I keep my drag set pretty tight but not locked all the way down. If I hit a huge hot fish I want it to slip a little rather than break my line. If I have to stop a fish that does take drag, all I do is put thumb pressure on the spool.

As far as line, the lightest I will flip or pitch with is 17 pound test Stren. If you need line lighter than this, it is probably not a flipping or pitching situation. I prefer to use 30 pound test DuPont Magnathin most of the time. This is a thin diameter yet very strong line and has given me excellent results. Lately I have also experimented with DuPont's High Impact line which really holds up great around cover where fraying becomes a factor. The oval lines like 7/20 and 14/40 are preferred by lots of anglers. Whatever line you use keep in mind that you still have to retie regularly. Even using these

In addition to the proper rod, a flipping/pitching reel such as the TD-1 Team Daiwa which has a flipping switch, is necessary for productive flipping tactics.

heavy test lines your knots fatigue and your line becomes frayed because of the heavy cover you are fishing. I try to retie after every fish I catch or after getting hung up. Flipping and pitching is intense, semi-complicated fishing and corners cannot be cut anywhere so your first step should be getting a proper rod, reel, and line.

Flipping Lures, Options and Colors

We have already talked about most of the lures I use flipping and pitching, but let me highlight and go into a little more detail about my favorites.

The jig and frog has been my #1 money bait. The bait I use the majority of the time is a 3/8 ounce jig with a Jr. Bo-Hawg

137

Frog. Keep in mind a flipping jig needs a strong weedguard and hook. This is not the place for light wire hooks. Also keep in mind the majority of people prefer 1/2 and 5/8 ounce jigs for flipping and pitching. If you remember the chapter on cold fronts and weather, however, you'll realize that you need different weights to obtain different speeds of fall which trigger bass. You also need different weights for certain cover situations. The heavier the cover usually the heavier the jig needed to penetrate it.

I like dark colors for the majority of my jigs--black, blue, chartreuse, green, brown, red, purple. They are all good colors but black is normally my base color with a few strands of another color. Black with blue and a black frog; black with chartreuse rubber and a black and chartreuse frog; black and brown with a brown frog. There are many color combinations. Figure out some colors for different water conditions and develop confidence in them. Pork trailers that will work well include the Strike King Pig Tail Trailers, the Sr. and Jr. Bo-Hawg Frog, and even the Pork-O with Diamond Dust.

Another great jig trailer, especially in warmer water, is the plastic crawfish. Some of these need to be cut down in length and made more compact at times but over all they make great jig trailers. I designed one called the "Pro Craw" for Bass Pro that you can put a rattle in. Others currently on the market that do a good job are the Big Claw, Hales Craw Worm, and Larew's Salt Craw. The colors are endless but some of my favorites are black with blue claw, fire and ice, junebug, black with chartreuse claw, and pumpkinseed.

Keep in mind that these baits are also great baits fished Texas rigged. A 1/4 to 1/2 ounce slip sinker with a 3/0 to 5/0 hook will do the trick. I always toothpick my slip sinker. When you toothpick, always slide the sinker on up after toothpicking

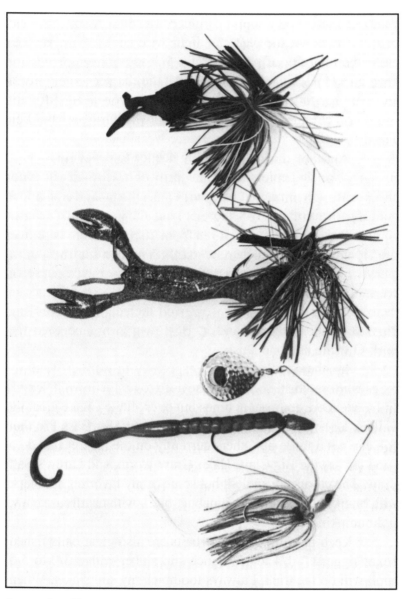

Any number of lures can be used for flipping although the most common are pig and jig, jig and plastic worm, and jig and plastic crawfish.

and cut away any possible bruised line that might have occurred from the toothpick. Then tie on your hook and rig your bait. At times I take a jig apart, taking the rubber skirt off and threading on a plastic crawfish. This gives a smaller profile look of just the crawfish with less pressure wave but also still gives you the good hooking results of my "Perfect Bend Jig Hook."

Another option of course is the plastic worm. These are great as jig trailers or by themselves. Normally in water temperature from 40 to 70 degrees I use the jig and frog and in temperatures of 60 to 85 degrees I use the jig and plastic craw or worm trailer. Temperatures from 70 to 90 degrees or over and I use the plastic worm by itself. You can see these temperature ranges overlap and they also vary some from region to region but they give you an idea or starting place.

Some worms that make great jig trailers are the Bass Pro's Tripple Ripple, 5-inch Gator Tail, or any other worm with built-in action.

In clear water I use smaller worms and in dirty water larger worms for greater pressure waves. Try to match your hook and sinker size with your worm. At times I have flipped worms with 1 ounce slip sinkers to get them down through heavy matted vegetation. Worm colors are basically the same as craw worm colors and are listed in the section on plastic worms. When fish are eating jigs or worms equally well, I usually flip or pitch the jig because it is a more compact bait and can be fished a little easier.

Also keep in mind that if you are fishing under real tough conditions or in an area with lots of fishing pressure, you might downsize to get a few more bites. This is also good if you are fishing an area that notoriously has small fish. I like to take a bait like the Kalin 5-inch grub or a large tube lure and rig them on a jig or use a Texas rig with them.

Another bait is the single spin spinnerbait. Here I use chartreuse with a gold colored Colorado blade in dirty water and white with a nickel or copper blade in clear water. A 3/8 to 1/2 ounce spinnerbait with a #4 or #5 blade works best. Lots of times I tip this with a #25 crawfrog of the same color. A plastic twin tail is also good and gives stability on the drop. Make sure you use a good swivel with the blade so that it turns easily on the drop.

These are the main baits I flip and pitch. Keep in mind that flipping and pitching are techniques of presenting lures so do not limit yourself. I have pitched topwater baits into hard to get to places and flipped spoons into holes as well, so be open minded. Develop confidence in these lures for fishing heavy cover and hang on.

Proper Presentation

Flipping is a line-in-hand, or limited distance technique where the amount of line is fixed. In other words, the reel is engaged and you're working with the same amount of line with each "cast." You control the distance between yourself and the target with your boat. If you're flipping 15 feet, use your boat to maintain the same distance to the target each time.

During a pitch, however, the reel is disengaged and basically an underhanded cast is made. The reel is normally turned to the inside and facing down. Pitching is more versatile and allows you to work a little further away.

One tactic I invented is the "loop pitch" which allows you to pitch a lure further than with the normal technique. Let out about 2 feet of line and let it hang down with the reel disengaged but your thumb firmly holding the line in place.

FLIPPIN' TACTICS

First step in flipping is to let out amount of line needed to reach target. With the hand not holding the rod, grasp the line and pull back about half the length.

Step 2--Swing the flipping lure back under the rod by lowering then quickly raising the rod tip.

Step 3--When the jig starts forward raise the rod tip and move the rod hand forward to increase the lure speed. At the end of the swing give a gentle flip to the rod.

Step 4--As the jig approaches the target, allow the line to slip through your fingers but do not let go of the line completely. Stop the jig just over the water surface.

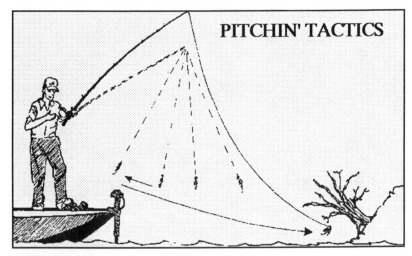

PITCHIN' TACTICS

Underhanded pitching is more versatile. Lower the rod tip then snap upward to pitch the lure forward releasing line from the reel as needed.

More pitching momentum can be gained by grasping the lure in one hand and pulling it tight, then releasing slingshot fashion as the reel is disengaged.

LOOP PITCH

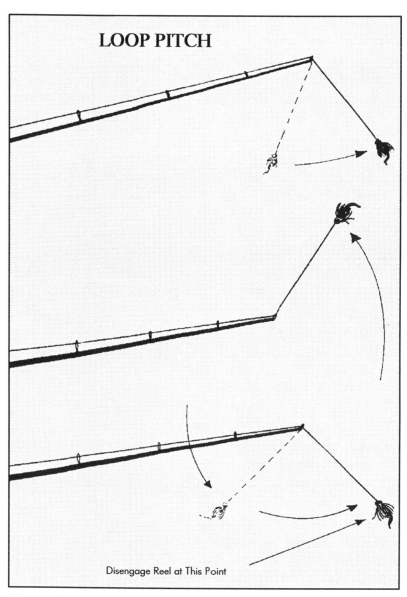

Disengage Reel at This Point

A loop pitch can also be used to gain momentum and increase pitching distance. Allow about two feet of line out, then snap the lure upwards and around in a 'loop.'

Give a sharp snap to make the jig rotate a full 360 degrees in a circle or loop, forcing the jig to shoot up toward you and then back down. Then proceed like you would in a normal under-handed pitch. All you're doing is building momentum with the lure by taking it in a 360 degree swing and releasing your thumb at the proper time which forces the lure to shoot toward the target.

In both flipping and pitching it is very important to make as quiet a presentation as possible. This takes practice but is very important to make the techniques effective. You are primarily dealing with shallow bass and the more natural the entry into the water, the better your chances of getting a bite especially from a big fish.

I learned to pitch and flip at home, standing by my couch in front of the TV. I put a coffee cup under some house plants on a table and by the end of the winter most of the plants were gone but I could hit the coffee cup every time! It's surprising how accurate you can get with a little practice.

A soft entry is important and the key is feathering the line to slow the bait just as it settles into the water. I let my baits fall on a semi-slack line so they fall straight down into the cover unrestricted. I'm still aware, however, at all times of what my baits are doing. Any time I'm not sure what my bait is doing, I set the hook immediately.

In flipping and pitching it is extremely important to have total concentration on your bait and what's going on around it. You need to watch your line for any tell-tale movements, you need to watch the cover you are fishing for any movement, and you also need to monitor your bait. You need to know if it hits bottom or if something stops it in the process. If a bush or reeds or anything shakes when you make a presentation, you need to be aware of it. If you make a good presentation this means a fish moved to get the bait rather than spooked. If you splashed the bait in, it probably means you spooked another fish.

I never check for a fish when any of this happens, I just drop the rod tip, take a couple of cranks to take up some slack, and set the hook hard. Normally they have the bait and this gives them no chance of feeling you and spitting it out. I do the same if my line twitches or moves sideways. Likewise if I feel the bait has stopped short of the bottom. When the bait does get to the bottom, pump it a few times, then bring it out and put it into the next likely looking bass home. Keep in mind that with these techniques a high percentage of strikes come on the initial fall of the bait.

The colder the water and the worse the condition, the longer you usually have to work the bait. At times I have shook a jig in a bush for a couple of minutes before a fish finally hit it. Naturally you have to have a good idea a fish is there to fish it that long. The thing that makes this technique so great is that your lure is in the strike zone the whole time it's in the water.

The rattle jig is really an advantage when you have to shake the bait in the cover to draw strikes. You can also put glass rattles in your plastic baits to help get strikes.

Another little trick is to flip or pitch the bait onto a log or piece of cover and ease it naturally into the water. At times I even pitch a bait on shore and then ease it in.

When and Where to Flip and Pitch

This is very important. I have seen people try to force these techniques when other methods would be more productive. Cover normally determines the technique you use.

Sparse cover and clear water certainly is not a flipping

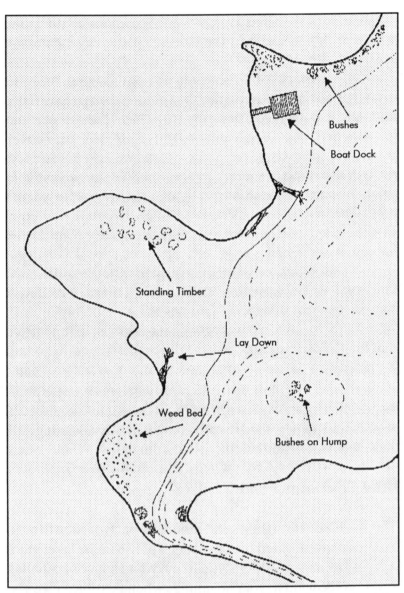

You need cover for productive pitching, the heavier the better. A wide variety exists including lay downs, log jams, standing timber, weed beds, boat docks, etc.

situation. The heavier the cover, the less it matters if the water is clear. In heavy cover you can usually flip without spooking the fish even if the water is clear. Stained or dirty water are desirable for these techniques but not mandatory. Keep in mind that the clearer the water and the sparser the cover, the farther you need to stay from the fish. This is where pitching is a must. If the cover is fairly uniform, I usually flip. If the cover is scattered or isolated, I normally pitch. An example of ideal flipping cover would be going down a grass line or reed line making one flip after another. If you see fish spooking, bushes shaking, or grass moving, you need to back off and start pitching. If you are still spooking fish, back off and start casting. Remember, however, the closer you can work fish the greater your percentage of landing them.

Let the fish and cover determine what technique you use. Normally you have to use a combination of flipping and pitching because cover is seldom uniform. The good, heavy cover fishermen are equally good at both. I have flipped and pitched chunk rock banks in stained water, I have flipped and pitched cracks in bluff walls, stumps, weed beds, reeds, bulrushes, docks, piers, bushes, trees, lay-downs, etc. The list goes on and on. Keep in mind the advantages and disadvantages of these techniques and use them accordingly.

Boat Positioning and Control

This is one of the most overlooked parts of good fishing. You may have located the best bunch of fish in the lake, but if you go crashing in on them, you'll ruin your chance of catching any. Use the wind to your advantage when possible. If you're fishing a flat of vegetation and the wind is blowing, let it drift you across while you flip or pitch in front of the boat. This is a quiet way to sneak up on spooky grass fish. On other types of cover I try to work into the wind when possible so that I can maintain better boat control and fish at the speed the cover dictates, rather than having the wind push me too fast. This also allows the boat to drift back away from the cover when you catch a fish so that you don't drift in and spook the rest.

Another thing I have noticed is someone takes a fish off a piece of cover and they are on high 24, going to the next piece. Keep in mind that at times a whole school of fish will hold on one little piece of cover. I remember one tournament where I caught 5 fish over 5 pounds off one stump. I caught two the first time I fished it, came back later and caught two more, then came back a third time and caught the fifth fish.

When flipping it is very important to keep the boat the same distance from the cover so that you never have to touch

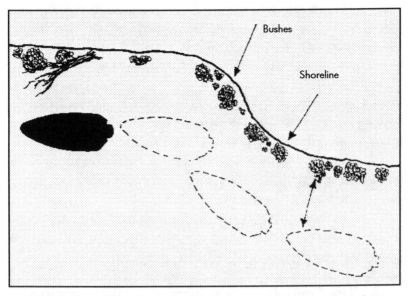

When flipping it is very important to maintain the same boat distance from the cover so you never have to touch the reel between flips.

the reel. Figure out the distance that works for you--not too close and not too far. Speed control is also important. It is better to go at a constant slow speed than in fast spurts. The quieter you are, the more fish you'll catch. I compare it to deer hunting--you need to sneak up on them.

I use a 12-24 Evinrude foot control trolling motor which allows me to have both hands free to concentrate on fishing. It is also a very quiet trolling motor which I am sure helps catch more big fish. A lot of fishermen (even pros) will never consistently catch fish flipping because their trolling motors are too noisy. Make sure the brackets are tight and the prop free from burrs and vibration. Think quiet.

In a tournament situation move fast enough to allow your partner plenty of fresh cover to flip or alternate pieces of cover or each take a side. This is important when fishing close and is just good sportsmanship. Also keep in mind where each fish is coming from to try and put together the pattern-within-the-pattern. They might be on bushes but are they on the windy side, calm side, sunny side, shady side, top of the bush, bottom of the bush, side, middle, green bushes, dead bushes, point bushes, isolated bushes, and on and on. You can do this with all types of cover situations. Definitely pay attention and analyze everything about every fish you catch.

Normally flipping and pitching is better on sunny days when fish are tight to cover. They are the most catchable during the 9 am to 3 pm period.

The combination of the flipping and pitching techniques has been very good to me over the years and can be good to you too! The average size of your fish will also increase.

Tip--Control your boat so you never flip or pitch in your shadow or cast a shadow where you intend to pitch.

Winning tournaments takes more than just knowing how to catch fish. It also requires observation of what other anglers are doing and then a winning strategy.

Chapter 6

TOURNAMENT STRATEGIES

Pattern Your Competitors

A tournament is really a contest between you and the bass. Other competitors, however, influence your success or failure so they must be part of the complete game plan. Always keep a file on each lake you fish. Keep all the information you can gather, tournament results, etc. You might see trends developing from your notes. Also keep in mind the publicity factor. If the last major tournament was won in a certain area you may need to avoid it because it will more than likely be covered up with fellow competitors. Some people are good at fishing in a crowd but I am not. I like to have an area to myself. I figure the more contestants I'm sharing an area with, the less my chances of winning. I can have a small school of fish to myself and win, but finish poorly by splitting up a big school with other contestants.

If you do have to share an area be observant. If a contestant works through your area before you, try to follow with a different bait or method. Also be aware of different anglers abilities.

When certain anglers weigh in large stringers, some of them normally fish certain ways and techniques. Some examples would be if Jimmy Houston weighs in a big stringer you might want to try a spinnerbait more the next day. If Rick Clunn weighs in a big stringer you might check out a crankbait on your fish. The examples go on and on. All good anglers are

A bass fishing tournament is actually a contest between you and the bass. You should, however, be extremely observant of what other competitors are doing.

capable of catching fish lots of different ways but always keep in mind their strong points. It just might give you a clue to putting more fish in your livewell.

The better you know your fellow anglers, the better your odds are to learn from them. At weigh-in if you see an angler weigh in a big stringer of pale colored bass you know they came from muddy or really deep water. If they are dark and well colored, they were probably shallow, clear water fish. Be observant and you can learn.

Capitalize on Winning Opportunities

A lot of anglers get in the position to win a tournament but never capitalize on it. Some never give themselves the opportunity to win. Some, just by their style of fishing, have little chance of winning.

First you need to analyze your goals in a particular tournament. Maybe you need to fish conservatively to guarantee a spot in a post season tournament or an honor like Angler of the Year. You might have areas that will produce enough fish to meet those goals but not enough to win. You realize that going in and concede to a goal less than winning. Lots of anglers are in financial situations that require just making the money in order to continue. These are all different situations and things to consider. Everyone needs to fish each tournament as smart as they can and determine what is needed to win.

All this, however, cuts down on the number of opportunities an angler has at winning a tournament. I try to fish each tournament to win. In order to finish first you can't be afraid of finishing last. Basically this means that because you are gambling or going for the win, you will occasionally fall flat on your face. You need to realize this going in as it is the down side of a winning style of fishing. However, if you don't give yourself the opportunity to win, you probably never will. The more you give yourself the opportunity, the greater your odds of winning. I attack each tournament this way. How much weight should it take. What areas have winning potential. What baits and patterns could allow me to win. The list goes on.

In a one day tournament a fisherman should hold nothing back. You go to your best spots and hit them for all they're worth. In a multiple day tournament you need to use strategy. Why weigh one big stringer one day out of a spot if you can weigh two or three or four average stringers and win because of consistency. Save a spot if it is inobvious and can give you a winning edge. Fish the obvious spots that others might compete for first. This automatically gives you an edge.

One of the keys to winning tournaments today is to fish the inobvious spots but save those for last. Fish the obvious spots other anglers might compete for first.

If you are in range of winning going into the last day, you need to make a big decision. Do you go back to the same fish and hope to hold your own and place well knowing you probably won't win. Or do you chuck everything and gamble on finding the fish that can win for you. Again this depends on the individual and the tournament. If might not be good business to gamble on winning or dropping out of the money if you can catch a few consistent fish, finish 2, 3, 4, or 5, and win some real big dollars. Calculate your odds and options.

I remember the BASS tournament at Chattanooga I won in 1985. I was in tenth place going into the last day and basically not in any shape to win it fishing where I was. I elected to make a long run in rough water to a spot that I had never caught a fish before. It, however, offered a good potential for winning. In practice I had charted a lot of bait fish with game fish below them laying in the river channel beside an underwater ridge. I could not get them to bite and was not even sure they were bass. The last day the wind was blowing hard and moved the bait in over the ridge and the bass followed. I gambled on this spot getting right and caught three fish that weighed 17 pounds and won the tournament. Obviously, I gave myself a winning opportunity and it paid off.

My theory is that you almost always go for it. It may be my nature, or the rewards of a successful career, but the thrill for me is going for the win. I'm just not satisfied settling for anything less. It can be hard for a lot of anglers to get in a winning position so the opportunities for gambling or going for the win are minimal. Establish your own goals and game plan and fish accordingly. If this includes winning, capitalize when you get a chance.

The Mental Part of Fishing (Negatives and Positives)

Fishing like any sport or occupation has emotional ups and downs. It is very important to realize this in the beginning and it will help you deal with it as you go.

First of all there will always be negatives in fishing. Patterns change, other people find your fish, weather changes, broken lines, lost fish, mechanical problems, the list goes on.

There should also always be positives. The key is consistently making more positives than negatives. The harder you work, the luckier you get. This basically means the harder you work, the more you eliminate the negatives and allow the positives to take over.

People with negative attitudes very seldom consistently

win or do well. Confidence breeds success. Always try to remain optimistic and think positive. Never give up even if things are not going right. Things can turn around in a hurry if you give them a chance. Try to become more consistent and eliminate as many of the negative things as possible. The better you fish, the better your attitude is going to be. When things are going totally right, it is very easy for anyone to keep on a positive attitude.

You need, however, to learn to maintain this attitude when things are not going so well. We all make mistakes at times but we should also learn from them and become better anglers because of our mistakes. If you go out with the negative thought that you won't do well, you probably won't. On the other hand a positive attitude keeps you fishing hard and basically forces you to have a good day. You are also thinking better on the water, constantly analyzing and trying to figure your best moves and opportunities. It is also easy to go from one mental attitude to another. A person might go out with a bad attitude and bang, a 5 pounder bites, his attitude changes, and he is off and running. On the other hand I have seen guys with great attitudes come apart after losing that 5 pounder and then let it affect the rest of their day, turning their positive attitude to a down beat negative.

Some people have trouble getting motivated and getting geared up with a good attitude. Other people are just naturally optimistic. Analyze yourself and keep in mind that your attitude will play a major part in your success as a tournament angler. Work on this part of your game and make it your strong point. Learn to handle the pressures of tournament situations positively and don't let this part of tournament angling that you can control alter your results in a negative way. Positive mental attitude means positive results.

The Partner Advantage
(Tournament and Practice)

Have you ever noticed that the same guys always draw bad partners. Did you ever think they may be the problem. Everyone has a different personality and some people just get along better than others. A partner for some anglers is the easiest excuse they can find for not doing well. Next to the weather, a bad partner ranks at the top of excuses and it shouldn't.

Partners need to get along and cooperate for the advantage of both contestants. Tournament rules guarantee equal opportunities for every contestant. Unfortunately anglers that don't work together really hurt their chances of success. The best rule to go by is to treat other people the way you want to be treated.

You may have a big name and lots of experience, but that doesn't mean your game plan is necessarily any better than your partners. Analyze your options and put your heads together to figure out how you both can catch the most fish. Above all, be totally honest. Never lead a partner astray and don't over estimate the amount or size of fish you have found. As far as baits and patterns, these also should be discussed so that your partner can be appropriately spooled and rigged. If you are on something unique, try to have duplicate baits for your partner.

All I do is fish for a living so I keep my equipment in tip-top shape and try to overcome the chance of losing a day because of something going wrong. I carry a spare prop, trolling motor, fuses, tools, locators, scales, measuring board, and catch-and-release, everything that can help guarantee my partner and I have a successful day on the water. My boats are

Partners can be good or bad, it's up to you. Next to the weather a bad partner ranks at the top of excuses but it shouldn't.

rigged for the gruelling needs of tournament fishing and I have lots of hours driving in all kinds of water. Naturally I prefer to use my boat and partners normally trust my judgment and allow me this opportunity. By the same token if I am not on fish, I concede this to my partner and if he is I automatically offer to ride with him if he feels his boat is equipped right and would be more at home in it. Common sense goes a long ways when two partners get together.

Some of the best friends I have were tournament partners. We gained each others respect fishing the tournament. Remember you are competing against the bass, not your partner. You should enjoy the day and work together to catch what you can. I never flip a coin to determine the boat we are going in or the fish we try for. I think a good discussion by two

160

people being honest with each other will yield more positive results than something as childish as flipping a coin.

For some this is an apparent ego trip just to say they are taking their own boat. I do not feel your true pros possess this attitude. The first time I drew Rick Clunn we decided to go to his fish in his boat and we each caught good stringers. The next time we drew out we went to my fish in my boat and had equally good days. Never once did flipping a coin enter either one of our minds. I have drawn Tommy Martin three times and all three times went with him to his fish in his boat. All three times I felt it was to my advantage and again I never thought of flipping a coin. The next three times we draw we may decide my fish are better and take my boat.

Lots of times I don't even charge my partners for gas when they allow me the privilege of taking my boat. I also tell them that they are welcome to use any of my tackle including rods and reels if they need to. This way they cut down on what they need to bring and you both fish better in an uncluttered boat. I also tell my partners that they are welcome on the front deck if they desire, and I try to make the entire day as fair as possible for both parties.

Getting along with partners is politics and good business. I have drawn partners that said they would be more than happy to go with me as I treated them great the last time or I treated a buddy of theirs fair. Believe me, the word gets out. If you treat partners wrong, the word will also get out and no one will look forward to fishing with you.

I have only drawn one angler that I thought was unprofessional and I had been warned in advance that if I ever drew out with him to get ready. He would make you flip a coin no matter what and would not listen to reason. Sure enough I drew him and he would not reason. He did not care if we fished my fish but wanted to have his boat on the water. Strictly an ego trip. I was forced to flip and lost. I caught a good bunch of fish and would have been able to help him catch more if I had my own trolling motor so I could do a better job of positioning the boat. He probably was more interested in boat racing than catching fish anyway. This was not a real fun day on the water because of his attitude and mine. I probably let his lack of reasoning and overall attitude affect me to where I was not a very good partner that particular day.

Don't worry about things like this and don't let them keep you from getting involved in tournaments. They are great places to learn and partners are great helpers and teachers. The majority of the partners you draw are level-headed, professional individuals. Just treat people fairly, honestly, and the way you want to be treated and you are on your way to a successful career in tournament fishing.

Also honor your partners fishing areas and never go back unless he invites you. And most of all, don't tell your buddies. The same goes with the patterns and baits he is using. Never do anything to jeopardize a partners future chances of doing well. Honor his requests and keep quiet.

Practice partners can be a plus but make sure first that the tournament rules allow the individual in your boat in practice. My son practices with me during some tournaments and I consider this an advantage. He is one of the best, most determined, hard-working anglers I have ever had in my boat and can definitely help establish patterns. It is mainly a matter

---

Tip--If you draw out the last day with someone that has a good shot at winning, let him do his thing and give him his chance. Your turn will come and you will appreciate the same courtesy.

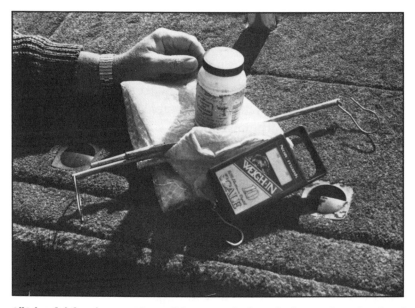

All I do is fish for a living so I keep all the essentials, the tools of my trade ready at hand including scales, measuring board, catch and release, etc.

of elimination and duplication. Eliminate the places, spots, patterns, and lures that don't produce and duplicate the ones that are most productive.

I try to have another person in the boat try different things. If I am throwing a spinnerbait, my practice partner could be throwing a buzzbait. If I am throwing a Pop-R, he might be throwing a Zara Spook. If I am throwing a jig, he should be using a worm. Once you start refining which bait is really producing, take it even further. Determine what size or color is best by using different combinations and comparing the results.

In the last couple of years a couple of anglers have resorted to using the help of local anglers in national tournaments. Having them show them the hot spots and best patterns. At present this is legal in pre-fishing practice, but illegal during actual tournament practice.

I personally feel that an angler should find fish with his own ability rather than being put on them. More pro's probably get led astray by these so-called local experts than actually get useful help. Everyone must establish his own standards and code of ethics but believe me you will have a lot more pride in winning with your own fish locating ability. You will also be a lot more consistent overall and will become mentally stronger and a more complete fisherman.

I pre-fished only one day in my career with a local because he said he could show me how to run through some dangerous areas. He ended up just wasting what could have been a useful day on the water. I do not mean to put down local anglers but in order to win you generally have to find a pattern or area that even they are overlooking.

It never hurts, however, to do some homework ahead of time on what the lake is doing--rising or falling, water temperature, tournament results, rainfall, dirty water, etc. are all important. This type of information can help you prepare to use your own fish finding abilities.

Determine the Potential of a Spot or Pattern

We don't need to talk a lot about this but I do think it is a problem area for some fishermen. One of the worst draws in the world is the guy that says I caught 30 bass out of this one spot in practice and we need to go there.

Obviously he has found a real good spot but more than likely he has ruined any chances of doing well by over fishing the spot. If he had caught a couple of good fish and then maybe bent his hook down he could have realized the potential and

One of the biggest mistakes beginning tournament anglers make is over-fishing a potentially good spot during practice. Check it, if it's good don't fish it.

then saved it for the tournament. The same with checking it.

I'll wait until the tournament to check a spot. Why take a chance of someone seeing you on a potential hot spot or sore mouthing another bass. I really do not even like showing my lures to bass needlessly. If I pull onto a bank and catch two fish right away, I may move down the bank a hundred yards or so and if I get a bite again, I realize that there is a good chance of lots of fish being there and I just save the spot.

Another example would be if I pulled into a cove with a bunch of flooded bushes and get bites in the first two, why fish them all--save them. At times you get fooled and there aren't as many fish in an area as you anticipate but that is the chance you just have to take in order to win. You must save as many bites as you can for the actual tournament. The more time you spend on the water, the more you can accurately analyze the potential of an area or an existing pattern.

Obviously if you are running a pattern of crankbaiting chunk rock points and you catch good fish on three of the first five points you figure you have something going. Rather than fish all the points just drive around and locate more potential spots just like these and gamble on their productivity for the tournament. The more patterns you establish, the better shape you'll be in as conditions and patterns change. I fish fast in practice and then slow down and work productive spots more thoroughly during the tournament itself.

Remember to stop and really analyze your spots and patterns. Try to figure to the best of your ability the potential of your spot or pattern without over executing. For every fish you catch off your spot or pattern in practice, it is more than likely one less fish you will catch in competition. At times some can be re-caught during the tournament but why hurt your odds if you don't have to. We all love to jerk and catch fish but in tournament practice be smart and develop a mental toughness when it comes to hook setting.

Equipment Really Can Give You an Edge

Lots of people have the attitude that if it does the job, fine, it will get them by. If you fish professionally this doesn't cut it. You need to surround yourself with the best possible equipment. You try to establish any edge you can and equipment is one way of doing it.

If you have to worry about whether your boat can handle rough water or whether your motor can make a long run, you are compromising your chances of winning. If you have to worry about your batteries running down or your

If you carry the proper, good equipment you will just naturally fish better. This includes good life jackets, two rain suits, spare props, and the tools needed for repairs.

trolling motor not holding you in the wind, you are in trouble.

Use good line that you have confidence in and rods and reels that continually hold up well. Use good lures with sharp hooks. Use a good vehicle to get to and from the tournament, and so on.

If you surround yourself with good products your mind will be at ease, you will naturally fish better, and be better prepared to win. You will have a true edge over someone that is fighting insufficient equipment.

Tackle and rods and reels speak for themselves. Carry what you need but do not over-clutter the boat. Also carry other necessities. Make sure you have good life jackets and a good rain suit. I also carry a spare prop for my big motor along with the tools to change it and also the tools to do whatever repairs I might be able to do on the water in case of a problem. Even though I run a very dependable trolling motor, I carry a spare one in one of my rod lockers. If I were to have a problem I could have a new trolling motor on in 5 minutes. I also carry a good push pole and everything that the law might require like a paddle, fire extinguisher, throw cushion, etc. I also mount a good measuring board on the floor of my boat so that I know where it always is. It also forces you to measure your fish in the bottom of the boat where if they flop they don't end up back in the lake.

I also carry plenty of catch and release chemical to guarantee that both mine and my partners fish will be in great shape for weigh in and alive to be caught again. I carry a spare locator, marker buoys, and a map. I have a good compass on

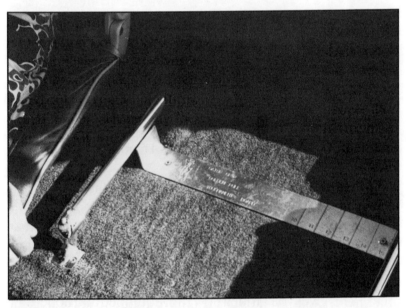

A good measuring board is essential for any bass angler, especially for tournaments. Fastened in the bottom of your boat, it is always available, and prevents losing fish.

To aid in the concentration needed for competitive tournament angling, everything should have a place in your boat and be well secured.

my boat and I have a hydraulic lift to help my boat and motor perform better in all conditions and to allow me to have access to more areas. I have a water pressure gauge along with all the standard gauges. I run three good batteries so that I won't ever run short of power. I have Rod Saver straps for my rods and use a trolling motor saver strap to help guarantee my motor staying put in rough water. I run a tandem trailer to give better trailering security and tow with a heavy-duty Chevy Suburban tow vehicle. I also check my hitch and look my rig over good every time I make a gas stop. Always make sure your lights all work and trailer brakes are also a good idea if you travel a lot.

This gives you an idea how I am equipped and hopefully it will give you some ideas on equipping yourself properly for more success.

Sponsors--Their Part and Yours

One of the questions I get asked more than any other at seminars and in letters and phone calls from hopeful anglers is how do they get sponsors. There are no easy answers but maybe some of the things I explain in this section can shed some light on the matter.

First of all it is best to understand what sponsorship is. Companies have advertising budgets to help increase consumer awareness of their products and these budgets can be used in a number of ways. Some companies elect to use television and/or the printed media with commercials to promote their products. Some elect to use tournament organizations as an exposure avenue. Some use the professional angler to get exposure. Some use all of these ways or any combination. In a way a professional angler is in direct competition for a limited amount of advertising dollars with TV, magazines, and even the tournaments in which he fishes. This means that if the angler wants some of this sponsorship money, he must be able to create a positive image with the consumer and be able to create favorable viewer impressions.

You are simply being paid to help a company sell products and you need to be aware of this in order to fulfill your part of the deal. Naturally the larger the deal, the more that is expected in return. If an angler is just getting started in tournament angling, here are some things to keep in mind.

First, put yourself in the position of your potential sponsors. What type of person would you want representing you. This should put everything in perspective. Appearance is very important. You must be neat and clean appearing. You may think your long hair and old holey jeans are great, but does the general public or a potential sponsor? Try to maintain a

Sponsors are a very important part of the success of any professional tournament bass angler. It requires many skills in addition to fishing to attract sponsors.

friendly, pleasant attitude with fellow competitors and fishing fans. Never publicly ridicule or blame equipment failure or other people for your lack of success.

Practice your speaking skills and try to become comfortable with a microphone in your hand. Everybody is nervous at first in front of a crowd but experience breeds self confidence and helps you overcome this. You might start out by speaking to local bass clubs to give you experience for public speaking and seminars.

Sponsors are very partial to anglers who are good speakers and have the ability to get up in front of a crowd and help promote their products. Success is also important. You can be the best public speaker around and present yourself very well and still not attract many sponsors if you can't catch fish consistently and finish in the money. By the same token you can be the best angler and winning everything and if your promotional abilities or credibility is questionable, you probably won't be able to attract a lot of quality sponsors.

If you can promote, have good credibility, and can really catch fish, you'll be very successful in this sport and attract plenty of quality sponsors. Also try to associate yourself with companies that have a good future and have products that you truly believe in and that won't hamper your success.

A company normally will start out furnishing you with products in exchange for promoting their products. As your fishing credentials and promotional abilities increase, so should the sponsorships. It may then progress to a cash retainer along with products. A good sponsorship means that it must be beneficial for both the company and the angler. If an angler builds his credentials and image to super star status, he then can warrant the big dollars in the sport. Multi-year contracts and an income from sponsors can run well into the six figure range. Most really good contracts are the result of working up the ladder with a given company. Loyalty goes a long way for both parties. As our sport has progressed so has the number of companies wanting to associate with and use the pro as an advertising tool.

The public likes to emulate or use the same products as a successful angler. Never jump from one company to another for minor reasons or a small raise. If another company in the same line offers you a lot larger deal, then you need to consider it. Always give your present company the opportunity to deal and analyze the long term results of a change. Loyalty means a lot but you must also keep in mind that this is a business and you owe it to yourself and your family to be as successful as you possibly can.

Don't burn bridges. Always remain professional in your dealings. Don't spread yourself too thin by trying to work with too many companies. Also make sure none of your sponsors conflict with each other. Some examples of possible sponsorships would be a boat company, a motor company, rod and reel, lures, line, vehicle, tackle boxes, marine accessories, etc. Also, keep non-industry related companies in mind. As our sport continues to grow so will the number of big non-industry companies that want to get involved.

Sponsorship is like fishing. The harder you work at it, the more successful you become. Lots of anglers get sponsorships and turn right around and lose them. Remember you need to get exposure for the company. Be willing to take the time to work with outdoor writers and the media. I spend a lot of days on the water with outdoor writers and photographers working on articles and shooting pictures. I'm not being paid directly to do this but it gets my sponsors and their products more publicity and helps justify their dollars.

Also, be aware of the little things like holding a fish up beside your motor so that it gets exposure along with the lure and the rod and reel. Maybe turn a boat seat so the name shows in a picture. Patches and hats are great ways to get exposure for companies. Make sure you are fair with the hats you wear as this is the key piece of clothing. Also make sure the sponsors patches are placed where they can get the most exposure. I think you get the idea. You need to give along with the taking. Nowadays you can make a good living from sponsors and you can also make a good living from consistent tournament winnings. But you can make a great living if you can successfully combine the two.

Catch and release must be practiced by all bass anglers, especially tournament anglers, if our sport and indeed, this great resource is to be enjoyed by future bass anglers.

Chapter 7

ON THE TOURNAMENT TRAIL

Lifestyle and Traveling (The Best Lakes)

A frequently asked question by outdoor writers and others is what really are the best lakes around the country. This is a tough one to answer and certainly depends a lot on variables. Timing is very important. A lot also depends on what type of fishing you truly enjoy. Lakes also go through cycles and one that was great a few years ago may be on a down cycle or vice versa. Let me give you some thoughts and ideas regarding certain lakes.

From the middle of March through April the Lake of the Ozarks in Missouri is my favorite lake--great fishing for both largemouth and Kentuckies.

Sam Rayburn Lake in Texas has treated me very good in tournaments and will always be a favorite. It has given up bigger bass every year, is a fun lake to fish, and offers a lot of patterns both deep and shallow. February and early March are my favorite times but you are subject to fronts and the lake can get rough when the wind blows.

Toledo Bend in Texas is always good but I like it best from the middle of January to the end of March. With the introduction of Florida bass, the giants should start showing up. If the vegetation remain stable, I predict the "Bend" could be one of the hottest lakes in the near future.

The Thousand Island area in New York can be fantastic fishing. This is especially true on the large bays of Lake Ontario for smallmouth when the season first opens. The middle of June to the middle of July is best (check for season dates). This is also a good time for largemouths in the St. Lawrence River. The largemouths seldom run much over 5 pounds but the fishing is good. The lake smallmouth run up to 4 pounds with a few larger ones.

Truman Reservoir in Missouri can be a very hard lake to learn but will always be a true favorite of mine. I guided there and it is a hard lake to consistently master, but it has a lot of big fish and when hit right can give up some giant stringers. Truman is good from March through November but is noted for being a great summer lake. When fishing drops off in most lakes it gets just right on Truman.

Kentucky and Barkley Lakes in Kentucky and Tennessee are great fisheries. Kentucky Lake has been hot lately because of the vegetation but both are good lakes with lots of good areas. They offer a variety of patterns and Kentucky Lake even has a good smallmouth population that is getting stronger. I like the May through June period which usually means fish in the bushes and willow trees.

Chickamauga Lake in Tennessee is another lake which has treated me great in tournaments. It had a reputation as a small fish lake but in reality holds some quality fish. The 72 pounds I weighed in during the BASS Pro Am should show the quality of the fishing. It has great grass beds, ledges, stump fields, and just seems to get better.

Guntersville Lake in Alabama is a true fish factory and has had lots of exposure the last few years. Grass is what made it good and I just hope that the fight to get rid of the grass doesn't also get rid of the good fishing. I look (unfortunately)

Everyone has their favorite lakes, and in naming some of mine I may have left out some of yours. Some may be like Truman, often fantastic and often frustrating.

for a down trend to this great fishery because of the uneducated eradication of the vegetation which breathed life into the lake to start with. Right now fall fishing on the grass mats is great using spoons and other grass baits.

Bull Shoals in Arkansas in April is good if it is high or normal. If it's high, spinnerbaiting and pitching jigs to bushes is very productive. When it's normal the Zara Spook will really produce. For those that also enjoy fishing deep on light line, fishing Bull Shoals is good year round.

Table Rock Lake on the Missouri/Arkansas line is a fantastic late winter/early spring lake for big fish. Stickbaits jerked around cedar trees and windy points produce well. The lake also has some good smallmouth. Late fall can also produce good Kentucky bass fishing. Grubs off long gravel points produce well.

Lake Mead and Lake Powell out west are beautiful lakes and offer some unusual scenery and a unique fishery. The fishing is tough most of the time and the lakes can require long boat rides, but I have always enjoyed fishing them. I have had some great Pop-R fishing on Lake Mead and if you enjoy stripers, the place is loaded. April is best for large fish but the real hot months can still produce good action.

Ohio River is not a good bass fishery in most pools although there are some good areas.

The St. Johns River is an overrated fishery but does give a few big fish.

The Potomac and James Rivers are pretty good tidal waters, and sometimes produce good fishing.

Buggs Island in Virginia is a very good fishery that can offer a variety of fishing. I have only fished it in the fall but I bet it's fantastic when the water is high in the spring.

Okeechobee Lake in Florida was a lake I hated until I

learned a little about fishing it. Now it is one of my favorites and a must for any serious bass fisherman to spend some time on. One day in a two-hour period I caught two fish in the 10 pound range and several between 4 and 8 pounds. It can be fantastic. January is my favorite month, but all year is good.

Naturally I have not listed all lakes but this gives you a glimpse of the ones I prefer and even a few that I really don't care for. I'm sure even the ones I don't like are favorites of some people and I don't mean to offend anyone or insult their fishing water.

The Contestants
(Superstars, Stars, Potential Stars)

We hear the name superstar used a lot in other sports to describe the highly successful and highly publicized individuals that star at what they do. Bass fishing also has superstars and as it grows in popularity, it will have more and more.

Each individual, angler, or outdoor writer has to determine in his own mind what category each angler falls in. A professional bass angler, in my opinion, has to qualify in several ways in order to reach the superstar category.

The person has to be a multiple tournament winner. A flash in the pan does not make a superstar. The person has to prove consistency and this takes several years; has to work well with the media and attract publicity; has to gain the respect of the industry,his fellow competitors, and the angling public. The list probably goes on but it still boils down to the individual.

You can take two people with the same credentials and one, because of desire and personality, will become a superstar and the other will just fall into the fishing star category. This is a very fine line and one that can be crossed back and forth depending on success and attitude. Bill Dance and Roland Martin were early tournament superstars and enhanced their image and publicity with TV shows. Other anglers like Jimmy Houston and Hank Parker have also combined tournament success with TV to reach the numbers of fishing fans.

The popularity of the sport and the media exposure it has received in recent years has given several anglers the opportunity to reach this level without a TV show of their own. Names like Larry Nixon, Rick Clunn, Gary Klein, and hopefully myself. Bassmaster TV has given us exposure all across the country and plays a big part in our success along with those great outdoor writers.

I hate to even mention names because where do you draw the line. In my personal opinion the difference in some cases between a superstar and a potential star is just time. A potential star can get hot and skip through being a star to superstar status in a short time with proper publicity. Guido Hibdon and Randy Blauket are two anglers that recently have had good success and have enhanced their careers. Other potential stars have faded from the scene. I think our sport is healthy but I think we continually need new blood with young people reaching for the stars. Maybe it is a real tribute to the ability of the established pros that we can continually hang onto the top spots and dominate the sport. I am not going to do a list and say these guys are the superstars, stars, and potential stars because it would do no one any good and it would just be my opinion. Most anglers know what category they fall in and hopefully we all are superstars in someone's eyes.

I have a lot of friends in the sport and whether they are technically superstars or not they are superstars in my book just for being the great gentlemen and sportsmen they are.

That is the neat part about our sport, success does not necessarily separate the anglers.

It is a pretty friendly bunch with common goals and respect. I don't know if people in bass fishing are more laid back and easy going or what but overall they are great people to call friends and associates. Most of the anglers truly care about the sport and the welfare of the bass itself. An example is Tommy Martin, a true star who could sit back, fish, and enjoy his success. But not Tommy. I have seen him spend countless dollars and his own time to try and better the sport for his fellow competitors. Others also fall in this category. Hopefully as the sport continues to grow and mature, the contestants can become even more united and push bass fishing to even greater heights.

The better we can make tournament fishing, the more potential stars we will see who will become stars of the future and eventually superstars. If you have a dream and the right work ethics, you already are a potential tournament star of the future.

The Promoters

Hopefully everyone involved in bass fishing is a positive promoter of the sport. Even when an angler is out fishing he can properly promote the sport by cautious sportsmanship and boat handling. Being in a tournament or owning a bass boat does not give you the right to drive carelessly or pull in front of someone else in a fishing spot. Someone out pleasure boating or crappie fishing has the same rights you do so respect them. The classier you act at the gas station, the ramp, or on the water, the more the image of bass fishing will increase.

Bass fishermen come from all walks of life but they

Promoters are a very important part of todays professional bass angling industry and one of the forerunners is Forrest Wood of Ranger Boats.

should all be involved in creating a fun, positive image for the sport. As individuals that is our responsibility. It is also our responsibility to protect the bass and the quality of its environment. We truly are watchdogs of the waters of this great country.

As tournament fishermen we have an even greater responsibility to make sure we take care of and handle our fish properly. All steps should be taken for successful release. Bass clubs and small tournament circuits are great if they respect the bass and employ strong measures to insure catch and release. If they don't, they should not get your participation because they are doing the sport a great injustice. A bunch of dead fish is not the image our sport needs. For those that don't tournament fish the same goes for dragging a big stringer of bass in just for pictures or inflating your ego and not being able to release them in good shape. There is nothing wrong if someone truly needs a few bass for food, but don't get carried away.

I like eating fish, but very seldom do I put a knife to a bass. I feel like I'm destroying my retirement plan every time I do. Other species like crappie do a better job of filling this need and are more prolific. Hopefully you can see that at whatever level you are involved in bass fishing, it is your job to promote the sport properly and protect this valuable resource. It is even more important for the larger tournament organizations because they get the most publicity and attention. We have had good promoters and bad promoters over the years. We are lucky a couple of the bad ones, in it only to make a fast buck, did not set the sport back.

On the positive side, everyone in bass fishing owes a debt of gratitude to Ray Scott. When Ray founded BASS (Bass Anglers Sportsman Society) I'm sure he had no idea the sport

Of course, professional bass angling would not be where it is today without the efforts of such promoters as Ray Scott, founder of BASS.

would grow to its present level. But thanks to the foresight of people like Ray Scott of BASS and Forrest Wood of Ranger Boats, the sport of tournament bass fishing has moved forward tremendously.

BASS has been the leader and set the standards that all other organizations should try to live up to. They initiated the fight against pollution and taught the nation the importance of catch and release. Because BASS has grown so large and established itself as the leader of organized tournament fishing, it also has a tremendous responsibility. It needs to continue to develop the sport and push for better and larger payouts so that a higher percentage of angling dreams can be reached.

As anglers we are never satisfied. We always want

bigger and better things for our sport. This is natural and BASS, now owned by Helen Sevier, has listened to and worked with the professional angler to enhance the future of the sport. It is great to participate in a BASS tournament because you know the payout is never in question and they are operated very professionally. Dewy Kendrick, Tournament Director for BASS, has done a good and fair job of running the tournaments and has enacted rule changes to further better the tournament fishing.

BASS has also helped the contestants establish themselves as public figures and stars with its magazine and TV show which both go by Bassmaster. I think that BASS will continue to be the leader in tournament angling because of its ability to promote and publicize the sport. I also think they will continue to better and move the sport forward. Let's all look forward to such efforts continuing in the future.

Other organizations like Operation Bass have done a good job over the years and have established themselves as running fair, honest tournaments for the weekend tournament angler. Recently they have branched out into national tournaments designed for the professional angler. Hopefully they will develop into another great avenue for the angler to be rewarded for his efforts.

Other tournament organizations will appear from year to year; some will make it and some won't. They all owe it to the anglers and the sport to run a fair, clean show. If they don't, they won't be around very long. Competition is good among promoters to help new ideas come forward and to help force larger and greater payouts. If everything is done right, and never jeopardized, the sport of tournament bass angling can be around for a long time, and maybe our children and grandchildren can enjoy this same great sport.

How to go About a Fishing Career

I think we pretty well touched on a lot of the important aspects in the first of this chapter.

I don't feel an angler can have success at a national level if he can't first win consistently at home. A good way to start is in bass clubs. I helped start a bass club in Seward, Nebraska, back in 1976 and this helped me decide if competitive angling was for me without investing a lot of money. I have some great memories of club tournaments.

As you have success at a club level, you can move on. I won the Nebraska State BASS Federation Tournament in 1978 and again in 1980. This gave me the opportunity to fish the National Federation Tournament and see how I could do on strange waters. I was happy with the results and gained the confidence to try a National BASS Tournament at Lake of the Ozarks in Missouri in 1980. Here I finished 20th and knew I had found something I wanted to continue in.

In 1981 I moved to the Lake of the Ozarks and started guiding on that lake and Truman. This gave me the time on the water I needed to develop my skills and learn how fish react to all types of situations. If you look at most of your successful anglers, they were fishing guides at one time or another. In 1982 I started fishing BASS tournaments full time and qualified for the Bassmaster Classic the very first year. In 1984 I won my first national and was on my way to a successful career.

I have been totally happy with the way everything has gone and I hope this shows you that it just doesn't happen overnight. It took me from 1976 to 1984 to get the type of true consistency and winning attitude I wanted. You also never stop learning or wanting to do better. There are a lot of things I still want to accomplish in tournament fishing and I will if I stay healthy.

I also read everything on fishing I could get my hands on. Great outdoor writers like Homer Circle fired up my desire to bass fish at an early age. Outdoor writers have done a lot to educate the bass angler over the years and can also help you if you desire a career in fishing. Work with your local media as it helps them and certainly helps you.

As you have national success, outdoor writers and the media are your greatest allies and career builders. Take the time to work with them and make their jobs easier. The exposure they can get you is critical for attracting sponsors and educating the public about who you are and what you have done. The press has been good to me over the years and I have enjoyed working with them and hopefully can call a lot of them friends. I hate to mention names but writers like Steve Price, Tim Tucker, Rick Taylor, Homer Circle, Louie Stout, Monte Burch, and of course lots of others--I owe a big thank you for all their support.

You can learn from these people and also learn from shows like Bassmaster and others on TV. Video's are probably the best learning tools of all because the pros actually show you exactly how to do certain techniques. Also try to fish with as many different anglers as you can so that you learn from all of them. Also, be open minded. You are never going to know it all or totally master this sport, so don't let your ego keep you from improving. The harder you try and the more knowledge you acquire will bring you closer to the high level of consistency we all desire.

I feel sorry for anyone who has to go through life working at something they don't really enjoy. I truly enjoy what I do for a living and hope that for health reasons or any other reasons, I never have to change. When you turn what is a sport or hobby for a lot of people into a successful profession, you become envied by a lot of people. I think for those who might be considering turning pro, it is only fair to show both sides of a career in fishing.

Yes, it is great to win tournaments and big paychecks. A good tournament angler can make some good dollars. Keep in mind however that for every pro making a good income from winnings, there are ten more struggling to just get by. With the cost of entry fees, tow vehicles, boats, general equipment, maintenance, gas, food and lodging, and a lot of other things, profits get eaten in a hurry.

I have seen anglers lose everything trying to become successful and this is very unfortunate. I would never discourage anyone from pursuing a dream, but dreams can be hard to realize. Keep things in perspective. Your family and their well being should be your first priority. Never give up everything to jump into tournament fishing. First, try a tournament or two on your vacation time not only to see how you do but also if you really like competition at that level. I have always said that until a person can consistently win or do well at a local level there is a very slim chance of doing well on a national level. I also feel it takes two or three years for an angler fishing nationally to really get established and learn how different parts of the country fish so that he can establish consistency nationally.

It is hard to be successful. It takes total dedication to the sport. You really have to work harder at it than any job you have ever had. Practice days are dawn till dark, get to the room and get things ready for the next day, study maps and analyze what you established, then get ready to do it all again the next day. I have fished a lot of tournaments where I only averaged 4 hours of sleep a night. The tournament days are actually the easiest part of tournament angling because the hours are the shortest. Tournament fishing can be a grueling lifestyle, especially when you consider the traveling.

At times because of commitments and personal appearances I have had to have someone drive my rig while I flew in but this is a rarity. Normally we tow our own rigs to the tournaments. Keep in mind that it is usually two days going to a tournament, six to eight days at the tournament and two more days driving home or to the next tournament. At times you will be on the road a month at a time. This can stress family situations unless financially you can afford to have your family with you. I really enjoy the tournaments but at times I regret all the traveling.

When I first started I slept in a lot of campgrounds and ate a steady diet of fast food. It was the only way I could afford to compete. My wife stayed home and worked so I could compete. Now she no longer has to work and gets to travel with me most of the time. We are very fortunate to be in our position, but it wasn't easy getting there.

You can see why I have mixed emotions about encouraging someone to jump into it. It is a very rewarding sport and I wish anyone who gets into it all the best. I do think, however, that they need to look at it carefully and decide if it is really for them. As the sport of tournament angling grows, so will the number of people that can maintain success.

Keep in mind that once you establish yourself you will also be traveling a lot doing seminars and personal appearances and spending time working with sponsors on projects and new product development. A real successful angler must learn to manage time carefully. You can lose all time for yourself and your family if you are not careful. Your time demands are great and this means you are very successful but you still need some days to enjoy without commitments.

A vacation for me is being able to stay home for a week and just enjoy my home and friends at Lake of the Ozarks and that is a rare treat. I also enjoy working with my black lab and hunting when I get a chance. Time does become precious. Because of all the demands you must truly enjoy it or you will burn out.

I think every successful angler has a responsibility to the sport that has treated him so well. It is our duty to get out on the show circuit and help make fishing more successful and easier for other people to promote and interest new people in fishing. To work on new products to help people catch more fish and enjoy their time on the water even more.

It is great to see all the tournament fishing fans nowadays. It is a special feeling to have someone ask you for an autograph or thank you for something you did or said to help them in their fishing. I have had people ask me if it didn't get old and a real hassle always being recognized, signing autographs, answering questions, etc. My answer to this is I hope they are still doing it when I'm 90. I feel most people are sincere and I enjoy answering their questions and doing the seminars to help them become better fishermen. And as far as signing autographs, that is a true privilege and makes a person feel very good when someone asks. I really cannot imagine any angler not feeling this way.

I guess I do indeed believe in dreams coming true. I had one and it definitely came true. The pot of gold at the end of the rainbow is there if you are dedicated enough and work hard. Keep in mind it takes total effort, the support of your family behind you, and some help from up above. Best of luck and I hope we draw out together.

GOOD FISHING!

Other fishing titles available:

MONTE BURCH'S
BLACK BASS BASICS

Describes successful techniques for largemouth, smallmouth and Kentucky bass in a wide variety of habitats including reservoirs, natural lakes, farm ponds and community lakes and creeks as well as rivers. Even bank angling is covered for those without boats. Also includes information on choosing and using gear, techniques for specific lures, understanding structure, where to find bass, and much more. 192 pages. $12.95 plus $2.00 shipping and handling.

Pocket Guide to SEASONAL
LARGEMOUTH BASS PATTERNS

Handy pocket guide book by Monte Burch is 3-1/2 x 5, 80-page book that fits in pocket or tacklebox to have when you need it—on the water. $4.95 postpaid.

Pocket Guide to SEASONAL WALLEYE TACTICS

Handy pocket guide by Monte Burch shows where to find walleye in rivers, lakes or reservoirs. 3-1/2 x 5, 80-pages. $4.95 postpaid.

Pocket Guide to OLD TIME CATFISH TECHNIQUES

Traditional catfishing techniques as well as the latest are covered by author Monte Burch. Rigs shown for all types of catfishing. 3-1/2 x 5, 80-pages. $4.95 postpaid.

TO ORDER: Mail check or money order to—

Outdoor World Press, Inc.
P. O. Box 278
Humansville, MO 65674-0278
417-754-8379